ALSO BY MARTHA STOUT

The Sociopath Next Door: The Ruthless Versus the Rest of Us

The Myth of Sanity: Divided Consciousness and the Promise of Awareness

ALSO BY MARTHA STOUT

The Sociopath Next Door: The Ruthless Versus the Rest of Us

The Myth of Sanity: Divided Consciousness and the Promise of Awareness

THE PARANOIA SWITCH

THE PARANOIA SWITCH

How Terror Rewires
Our Brains and
Reshapes Our
Behavior—and How
We Can Reclaim
Our Courage

MARTHA STOUT, Ph.D.

SARAH CRICHTON BOOKS
FARRAR, STRAUS AND GIROUX
New York

Sarah Crichton Books
Farrar, Straus and Giroux
19 Union Square West, New York 10003

Distributed in Canada by Douglas & McIntyre Ltd.
Printed in the United States of America
First edition, 2007

Library of Congress Cataloging-in-Publication Data
Stout, Martha, 1953–
    The paranoia switch : how terror rewires our brains and reshapes our
behavior—and how we can reclaim our courage / Martha Stout.— 1st ed.
        p.   cm.
    "Sarah Crichton Books."
    ISBN-13: 978-0-374-22999-3 (hardcover : alk. paper)
    ISBN-10: 0-374-22999-6 (hardcover : alk. paper)
    1. Paranoia.   I. Title.
    RC520.S76 2007
    616.89'7—dc22

                                                                    2007019750

Designed by Debbie Glasserman

www.fsgbooks.com

10 9 8 7 6 5 4 3 2 1

With more love than I can say,
I dedicate this book to my daughter,
Amanda Kielley

Let me make the superstitions of a nation and I care not who makes its laws or its songs either.

AUTHOR'S NOTE

The descriptions of my patients in *The Paranoia Switch* do not identify individuals. All patient names are fictitious, and other recognizable features have been changed.

Many of the people, events, and conversations presented here are taken from my twenty-six-year practice of psychology. However, many of the patients and circumstances portrayed on these pages are composite in nature; that is to say, each case represents a great many individuals whose characteristics and experiences have been adopted conceptually, carefully altered in their specifics, and combined to form an illustrative character. Any resemblance of such a composite character to any actual person is entirely coincidental.

CONTENTS

One   **HOMESICK WORLD**   3
The Walking-Around Anxiety Test

Two   **HOW TERRORISM WORKS**   21
The Contrast Effect from Hell
Orange Is Forever

Three   **THE DAY THEY CAPTURED CAT STEVENS**   45
Fear and the Human Brain
Yellow Ribbons and American Flags

Four   **FEARING AS ONE**   63
The Brain and the Dawn of Emotion
Limbic Resonance
Wynn Wins
The Trillion-Dollar Question

Five   **THE LIMBIC WARS**   91
The Japanese Are Coming
The Russians Are Coming
The Six Stages of a Limbic War

Six   **THE TERRORIST IN THE CLOSET**   117
The "Syndrome"
How to Rate a Crystal Coffin
Freedom Day

Seven   **FEAR AND THE SOUL OF A NATION**   145
        Red and Blue Genes
        Divided We Fall

Eight   **WHY WE CANNOT SEE THE DEVIL**   169
        Ten Behavioral Characteristics of Fear Brokers

Nine   **HOMELAND SECURITY**   187
        Courage

        Notes   203
        Acknowledgments   215
        Index   217

THE PARANOIA SWITCH

ONE　HOMESICK WORLD

Of all the tyrannies on human kind,
The worst is that which persecutes the mind.

—JOHN DRYDEN

Would you like to feel safe again in your own country?
If your answer is yes, like most people's, then you are personally involved in a struggle even more crucial than the war on terror. Though you probably have been only dimly aware of your situation, you have been fighting this battle for a number of years now, and the outcome of your private crisis will affect your future, and your children's, even more fundamentally than the success or failure of global terrorism. It is a struggle that your ancestors, from nearly all countries, have been through many times before, after man-made tragedies during the last five thousand years or so. Too often, they have lost the fight, but some-

times, by the skin of their teeth—and just well enough to keep human society going—they have endured. And here we are, doing battle with it once again.

Let me show you what I mean.

Spend a moment—and it will take no longer than a moment in this case—searching for some memories. What were you doing on the morning of September 11, 2001? This is an easy question to answer, is it not? You can recall precisely. What was your first thought when you discovered the news about the World Trade Center? Where were you? If you have children, where were they? Where were your other family members? Your closest friends? Whom did you speak with first? How did you feel on that day?

I imagine that you have immediate and extremely vivid memories to answer most, perhaps all, of these questions. Those of us who were adults or adolescents on September 11, 2001, will carry these memories to our graves, in a way that far exceeds our normal capacity to remember most things. We will be able to recall small details—the weather where we were, what we had been about to do but stopped doing, exactly which telephone we picked up—as if we had tiny videotapes in our heads.

But now search for another memory. Try to recall something—anything—about the morning of September *10*, 2001, a mere twenty-four hours earlier. What were you doing then? Where were you? Where were the people you love? How did you feel on *that* day? Most of you will be unable to answer a single one of these questions. I know that I cannot.

Less specifically—which, by rights, should be much easier to remember—what was life in general like for you during the summer of 2001, *before* the disasters? Overall, what kind of mood were you in? What were your major plans for that fall and winter? What projects did you have going? What were you dreading and what were you looking forward to, back then? Is it difficult to recall what life was like before international terrorism arrived in the United States? Even when you stop and concentrate, do the memories feel a little equivocal?

It is disproportionately hard to remember our lives as they were prior to the catastrophes of September 11, 2001. We can recall many of the most prominent objective events of our pre-2001 existence as well as ever, of course, but we know that the psychological fabric of our lives was somehow different, that we *felt* a different way, that we were, in effect, different people before the reality of terrorism was force-fed into our consciousnesses. And our memory of this is foggy, dim, and keeps slipping away when we try to hold it still for reflection. We simply cannot reconstruct the way we used to feel, and really, it is impossible to remember exactly *who we were* before those indestructible towers were obliterated.

We felt happier then. We felt safer. We were more trusting, less paranoid. We were . . . What were we?

We can recall 9/11 vividly, and are hard pressed to remember ourselves well before that day, because, on September 11, 2001, and in the years that have followed, fear has altered our very brains. The "fear switch" in our brains was pushed—pushed suddenly and very hard—by the attack, and has been pressed over and over again, though more subtly, in the years since that initial group nightmare. From neuropsychological research, we know that the traumatized brain houses inscrutable eccentricities that cause it to overreact—or, more precisely, *mis*react—to the current realities of life. These neurological misreactions become established because trauma has a profound effect on the secretion of stress-responsive neurohormones such as norepinephrine. Such neurohormones affect various areas of the brain involved in memory, particularly a part of the brain called the *limbic system*. Certain aspects of our memories are weakened in this way by psychological trauma, and certain other aspects become disproportionately powerful. In other words, for many of us, the functioning of our gray matter may actually be changed at this point, making it difficult for us to reconstruct memories of exactly how we were, and how we used to feel, though we were substantially different but a few years ago—and of course, making it impossible to *forget* the traumatic images seared into our brains. We cannot remember ourselves clearly; still, we feel strangely homesick for *the way we used to be*, whatever that was.

Even now, some years later, we are a great deal more anxious, cautious—and we do not like it. We snap at the person who stands a bit too close to us in the airport baggage line. Or, contrastingly, we warmly thank the security agent as he confiscates our fingernail scissors, because we are frightened of the inscrutable "others" who might be trying to bring more sinister cutting tools aboard the plane. We complain wistfully that we cannot allow our children to travel the neighborhood so freely as we did when we were young. With bated breath, we watch a lot more television news than we used to. And we reminisce about the good old days, when worrying about the likes of a little manicure scissors would have been simply laughable, although those days are becoming foggier, even dreamlike, in our minds.

In a world not at all lacking in traumatic events, how did those particular acts of terrorism manage to burn so deeply into the very biology of hundreds of millions, in what seemed like

less than a heartbeat, leaving us homesick for the way we had
been feeling just the moment before? After all, personally, very
few people knew anyone who perished in New York or Washington, or in the hijacked planes. When we think rationally
about our individual experiences, many of us can identify losses
that were closer to us, that have caused us more personal pain
and grief than did the events we saw only in pictures on that day,
images that nearly all of us were viewing from a great geograph-
ical distance. And in truth, on many occasions prior to 2001,
beginning in our very first history class in grade school, most of
us had already heard stories of objectively greater mass death and
mayhem. Still, 9/11 grabbed us by the throat like nothing else.
It changed us emotionally, behaviorally, spiritually. It caused
people of conscience to fear for the future of the whole human
world, and to wonder, sometimes subliminally and sometimes
quite consciously, what the true nature of that world might be in
the first place. Were humans basically good and decent beings,
and making slow but steady progress, two steps forward and one
step back, toward a higher civilization, perhaps symbolized by
the Twin Towers themselves? Or was the human race hopelessly
vengeful and violent, and headed for nothing better than the
ashes and dust of its own self-destruction?

We live our lives in our heads and in our hearts. We live for
our dreams, and on faith. Even scientists live on faith, though it
may be only the tacit (and distinctly unscientific) belief that
something about human beings makes them worthy of continued survival. September 11, 2001, made us question all that—
our dreams, our faith, our worthiness to survive on this
otherwise hospitable blue and green planet. And there simply is
no greater fear, or primal shame, than the one that speaks to us

of the End, the one that whispers, You do not deserve to be here—you are about to be banished by fire from your home.

For a moment, we all glimpsed the end, not just the end of our individual existences, but the possibility of the termination of humankind. As I describe in *The Myth of Sanity*, an event is officially "traumatic" only if it opens in the mind a corridor to the apprehension of our essential helplessness and the possibility of death. In this fashion, and in a big way, 9/11 officially traumatized nearly all of us.

For more than twenty-five years, I have been a psychotherapist for people who have survived psychological trauma. I have studied how trauma alters the mind and the brain itself. I have witnessed the suffering and the triumphs of hundreds of patients, and have written about the ways in which people can heal the damage done to them. And I feel an increasing urgency to tell the psychological victims of terrorism that they too can recover. The process of recovery from trauma can be divided into four components, and so this book, as well, is composed of four parts. First, I will provide you with a way to assess how much you personally are struggling with fear and anxiety. Next, we will address head-on the phenomenon of terrorism—its effects on us, its realities and myths, its likely time frame—just as a patient in therapy would come face-to-face with the realistic memory of her or his trauma. In the third portion of the book, I will describe how to protect oneself successfully against future perpetrators, who, in this case, are the leaders and would-be leaders who practice the politics of fear. And finally, I can tell you how to plan for a more serene future, one that includes hope, the very hope that terrorism is designed to steal from a nation of people.

Terrorism's anti-hope strategy was instantly successful in the United States. Immediately after the 2001 attack on the World Trade Center and the Pentagon, a Pew Research Center survey found that eight out of ten women and six out of ten men felt depressed. This means that, in the space of one morning in September, four fifths of all American women and three fifths of all American men were thrust into psychological depression. The people who were interviewed described recurrent unwelcome images of the horrifying events, replaying in their heads. And research on national samples in the United States, reported in the *New England Journal of Medicine*, revealed that, three to five days after the attack, 44 percent of ordinary Americans reported at least one clinical symptom of post-traumatic stress disorder (PTSD). These symptoms included (among other disturbing experiences) nightmares, dissociative reactions, impaired concentration, exaggerated startle responses, panic attacks, and shattered self-confidence. In other words, closing in on half of all Americans were, to a greater or lesser degree, suddenly behaving like psychological trauma patients.

Even those of us who did not show clinical signs of PTSD felt acutely guilty when we listened to happy music, or read books irrelevant to the catastrophe, or went to purely entertaining movies. And so, for a while, many of us stopped, almost completely.

Two months later, a *Los Angeles Times* poll indicated that 31 percent of respondents felt their personal sense of security was still "a great deal" shaken. This poll emphasized that the size of the group of Americans reporting a lost sense of security had not diminished appreciably since the first few days after the attack. About one in five of the Americans questioned in November 2001 actually believed they would "likely" be hurt or killed in a terrorist attack, such as the bombing of a building or a plane, and one in four were convinced they would be hurt or killed by an act of bioterrorism.

The attack, along with the media reiterations of it, had dramatic effects on our physical health as well. Study findings presented at the 2002 Scientific Sessions of the American Heart Association showed that, for individuals with defibrillators implanted surgically because of preexisting heart conditions, life-threatening heart rhythms more than doubled in the month after the attack. The AHA researchers speculated that a preoccupation with media coverage may have had as much to do with causing the arrhythmias as the events themselves. Supporting this speculation, most post-9/11 studies have found a strong association between media exposure and post-traumatic stress disorder, demonstrating that stress reactions to the attack were and are more common in people who watch a lot of television.

In 2002, at the one-year anniversary of the attack, a CNN/*Time* magazine poll reported that 30 percent of adult Americans—nearly a third—said they still thought about 9/11 every single day. And perhaps the most troubling finding of all, in its implications for the future, concerned a group of people not even born at the time of the attack. Scientists from the University of Edinburgh, in the UK, and the Mount Sinai School of Medicine, in New York, followed the infants of thirty-eight women who had been pregnant while at or near the attack on the World Trade Center. The study, published in 2005 in the *Journal of Clinical Endocrinology and Metabolism*, reported that when they were a year old, the babies of those mothers who had developed post-traumatic stress disorder showed low levels of the stress hormone cortisol. Reduced cortisol levels have been linked with vulnerability to post-traumatic stress disorder. The results of the study present the far-reaching suggestion that maternal post-traumatic stress disorder may have transgenerational effects beginning when a child is in utero, and the researchers are following the babies as they grow up, to see whether they will go on to develop psychological disorders of their own.

Pre-9/11 research had already shown that the grown children of World War II Holocaust survivors tended to have low levels of cortisol, and scientists had concluded that this condition was the eventual result of the traumatic stories told to the offspring by their parents. But now, the age of the offspring involved in the post-9/11 study—a year or less—strongly suggested that some part of the trauma transmission mechanism predated birth, and was, in fact, biological.

The attack on 9/11 psychologically devastated us and our children, more even than we realized at the time. On account of it, we were and remain vulnerable, as individuals and as a population. And so, enter the advantage-takers, beginning before we had even finished counting the dead and continuing to this moment, the worst of the politicians and the greedy and the just plain ignorant, from the level of our townships and cities to the unreachable echelons of national and international power.

Juxtaposed with the immensely beautiful acts of the firefighters and police and other rescue workers, the selflessness of so many doctors and nurses and engineers and anonymous citizens, and the mystically poignant outpourings of grief and compassion and solidarity from people all over the world, came the increasingly frequent news reports of the Ground Zero con artists and their astonishingly selfish agendas. From our televisions, we heard the voice of a young man shouting, "Bicycle tour! Guided tour of Ground Zero! Only ten dollars!" And we learned about the hustlers on Manhattan street corners who approached shell-shocked citizens to solicit "contributions" to nonexistent charities, and the would-be identity thieves who collected the Social Security numbers of the missing from the bereaved, assuring them that the information would be helpful in identifying bodies.

In a letter to the 110th Precinct Community Council, police captain Natale Galatioto assured the people of his Queens, New York, neighborhoods, "We are working hard not to give our streets back to scoundrels who may see this tragedy as an opportunity."

Somewhat more subtle were the politicians, some sincere and some merely selfish, who used our fears to secure our allegiance (and our votes). Fear platforms typically implied something along the lines of "Vote for me, or the terrorists will strike us again!" Perhaps the most hotly debated American example of "fear politics" was then Vice President Dick Cheney's direct remark at a town hall meeting in Des Moines, Iowa, on September 8, 2004: "It's absolutely essential that eight weeks from today, on November 2, we make the right choice, because if we make the wrong choice, then the danger is that we'll get hit again, and we'll be hit in a way that will be devastating from the standpoint of the United States." Speeches playing on our existing fears were made by candidates on both sides of the American political fence, and we accumulated a new vocabulary of menace to rival any apocalyptic novel: weaponized anthrax, Office of Total Information Awareness, orange alert, terrorist cell, dirty bomb, axis of evil, WMDs, shock and awe, perpetual war.

A separate struggle with terror began to emerge, between the frightened and the scaremongers, between the genuinely caring majority and the selfish impostors—between reason and bewildering anxiety, American idealism and the unthinking fight-or-flight instinct, our newfound sense of global unity and the primitive lust for revenge. And for a while, whatever victories we claimed in the official war on terror, it seemed that this separate struggle, the one in our minds and in our society, was a fight we were losing. We bought bottled water and books on survivalism and new surveillance systems and community police stations. We trimmed financing from literature and the arts, medical research, environmental concerns, and our children's community schools. Terrified and confused, we questioned our ideals and abandoned many of them willy-nilly: our privacy and perhaps too many of our liberties, our sense of tolerance and fair play, and a majority of the painful, important truths we had learned from waging past wars. Then, frustratingly, almost unbelievably, subsequent research informed us that all these contortions of our values and all these costly sacrifices had not served to make us one whit safer. And to our shock, in natural disasters later on, we realized that our protective infrastructure had been weakened rather than strengthened.

As it turned out, we needed some hope and clear thinking, and some encouraging, pragmatic leadership, much more than we needed stored supplies of duct tape.

With the understanding sometimes available only in retrospect, now we are beginning to realize that wrestling with our fear, and with those who would profit from our fear—even more than the war on outside terrorists—is the crucial struggle, the one that will more fundamentally affect our future and our children's. It is not that protecting ourselves, especially at home, is unimportant. On the contrary, now more than ever before, we need to do what we can to make our homeland safe—our cities and our transportation systems, our power plants and our food supplies. It is that these important tasks are much better done rationally, bravely, and well. Fear makes us frantic and alarmingly inefficient. And by definition, fear allows the terrorists, of all stripes, to win. Fear beguiles us further and further away from ourselves and our ideals, and from our priceless sense of security in our home—both our national home and our somewhat abstract human one. Fear is more widely destructive than anything we can be afraid of. Fear makes us do things we would not otherwise do.

And fear is contagious. As I will discuss in detail in later chapters, scientists have begun to study a fascinating brain process called *limbic resonance*, by which a part of the brain mentioned before as having to do with emotion and memory—the limbic system—can draw the emotions of a pair of people, or even a larger group, into congruence. One brain "tugs" on another to feel loving or joyful or angry or peaceful or hostile—or fearful. To use recognizable examples from the psychiatrist and writer Thomas Lewis, limbic resonance is what makes it more exciting, more romantic, or more teary-eyed to watch a movie with another person, rather than alone—and in less sanguine circumstances, it is what "sends waves of emotion rolling through a throng, making scattered individuals into a unitary, panic-stricken herd or hate-filled lynch mob." Our limbic systems act as the antennae for and the broadcasters of our emotional states, and they make our affections, our hostilities, and our fears invisibly and wordlessly communicable.

The implications of limbic resonance for terrorism and fear politics are clear and alarming. Due to the nature of our neurological wiring, one terrorist act—or a single scaremongering leader—can electrify a large group of people with fear as if they were a circuit. This can happen rapidly, with no need for logical reasons, and without anyone understanding at all what has happened to the crowd. And, reverberating, mirroring itself again and again, the same charge of fear and paranoia can last for a very long time, more than long enough to embroil the group in irrational, disastrous decisions and acts that cannot easily be undone when the situation is finally calmed.

This vicious circle is terrorism's cruelest manipulation of the human mind. We in this country "discovered" it, agonizingly, beginning in the year 2001. But really, it is universal, and thousands of years old. It feeds voraciously on itself, and repeats and repeats. Even the unambiguous lessons of history regarding conflict and violence seem to be no match for this self-sustaining cycle of fear and irrationality, once it has been put in motion.

Can we ever learn to protect our minds—and our very brains—from terrorists of all kinds, from the petty sociopaths who violate our personal lives, to the various fundamentalists and the power-hungry who commit mass violence, and the leaders who, for their own gain, would amplify our group fears into hatred and war? In this book, you will read a positive answer to this question. It has been my privilege, as a behavioral scientist and a therapist for trauma survivors, to work closely with people who have faced and overcome attacks and colossal fears in their individual lives. They get past their personal terrors, and then they rediscover themselves. I write this book, with its optimistic conclusion, based in part on my respect for these courageous people. I think that most of us, these days, could benefit from certain aspects of the trauma therapy they have braved, and will present my ideas about how such a societal trauma therapy might work. And in no small measure, I write this book on faith, albeit the faith of a scientist. I believe that, as individuals and as a species, we will ultimately win this psychological struggle, which is both very old and brand-new. Maybe not all of us—but enough of us—will one day turn away from those who try to control us with our fears. Come with me and let us talk about how we are going to triumph in this ancient human contest, about how we are going to get past the real war on terror and find our way home—that secure and dignified place that most of us, all these months and years, have been longing for with all our minds and hearts.

As I have mentioned, the first step in any such recovery process is to assess the severity of the problem. If you are interested in exploring the level of your own general anxiety in this new age of terrorism and fear politics, you are invited to take a brief self-evaluation that I call *The Walking-Around Anxiety Test*, meaning that the test gauges the amount of anxiety you tend to carry around with you on an ordinary day. Answering these questions does not by any means constitute a clinical evaluation, nor will it sort out how much anxiety you are feeling due to terrorism as opposed to other issues. The self-test is intended only to give you a sense, in broad outline, of how anxious you are at this point in time. The questions here are some of the ones I often use in therapy evaluations, to help provide me with an initial impression of a new patient's level of anxiety or fear in his or her day-to-day life. Answering them can give you some idea of the degree to which your own limbic system is broadcasting anxiety, or perhaps even receiving it.

Please be forewarned that your results may surprise you.

THE WALKING-AROUND ANXIETY TEST

Answer yes or no to each of the following questions. Try to answer each question based on your feelings and behavior *this week*.

1. When you sit still for a while, do you tend to have a "nervous habit": tapping your foot, or fidgeting with your hands (doodling, nail-biting, pencil-tapping, hair-twirling, etc.)?

2. Within the last week, have you had a dream you would describe as a nightmare?

3. Does your mind tend to "go blank" temporarily, or wander away from conversations?

4. Are you jumpy?

5. Within the last week, have you noticed a time when your breathing was shallow, or when you "forgot" to breathe for a moment?

6. Within the last week, have you noticed a time when your heart was racing, even without exercise?

7. Right now, are your palms sweaty?

8. Do you frequently notice that your muscles have gotten tense, particularly around your eyes, or in your neck or back?

9. Within the last week, has anyone told you to calm down, or to "stop worrying," or the like?

10. Is it hard for you to stop worrying?

11. Would you say that your mind is filled with worries more often than it is not?

12. At night, is your mind crowded with thoughts, making it difficult for you to fall asleep?

13. If you had not read or heard the news for a day (newspaper, radio, TV), would you feel uneasy?

14. Within the last week, has anyone said that you were being tense or irritable?

15. Within the last week, has there been any occasion when you worried you might lose control of yourself, or embarrass yourself?

16. When you are around a lot of other people, do you tend to feel trapped?

17. Does your mind tend to dwell on bad things that happened in the past?

18. Within the past week, has there been any occasion when you felt uneasy about leaving home?

19. Does there tend to be an unwanted thought or picture in your mind that you have trouble getting rid of?

20. This week, have you been going back to check on things more than once (locks on doors, burners on stoves, etc.)?

21. Do you often feel restless, or as if you are supposed to be doing something else?

Now count the number of your yes answers. If you answered yes to seven or fewer of the questions, it is likely that your general anxiety level is not causing you much discomfort. If you gave a yes answer to between eight and fourteen of the questions, your anxiety level may be somewhat elevated. Perhaps you experience this as mild to moderate discomfort in your day-to-day life. This level of anxiety is not alarming; still, it may be placing unnecessary limits on your happiness. If you answered yes to fifteen or more of the questions, your anxiety level is likely to be making you very uncomfortable, and in view of this preliminary information, you may want to allow yourself to seek professional help with your anxious feelings.

Whatever your score is, I recommend that you make a note of it, and then take the test again after you have read the remainder of the book.

More than anything, I want to wake you from your numbing anxieties about this strange new world, and to give you some rational hope for the future.

TWO

HOW TERRORISM WORKS

No one can terrorize a whole nation,
unless we are all his accomplices.

— EDWARD R. MURROW

As Americans, we tend to ignore a crucial aspect of the problem of terrorism, which is, simply, that terrorism does not always work. From the face of it—the violence, the bloodshed, and the immediate despair—we tacitly accept that any sizable terrorist act always works to complete the aims of the terrorists who contrived it, but this is not the case. Looking a little beneath the surface, we discover the surprising fact that even lethal terrorism is not always successful.

Since 2001, our leaders, some of them horrified and morally outraged, and some of them merely opportunistic, have told us repeatedly that terrorists attack *because they hate us*, and many of us have come to accept radical animosity as the primary motivation behind terrorist acts. This gigantic resentment in the hearts of terrorists is presumed to result from the political freedom and material wealth of the citizens of the United States, versus what we perceive as the complete lack of freedom and the cultural failure and poverty of those who would attack us. Since the emotional goal of hatred is to hurt, and since terrorists always inflict injuries, Americans who view hateful resentment as the main motivator of terrorist acts tend to see terrorism in oversimplified terms. The question "Did this particular act of terrorism work?" is never asked, because such a question makes no sense within our belief system. According to our assumptions, terrorism *always* works, because it hurts us, and therefore it satisfies— temporarily, anyway—the hatred and jealousy of a category of people we see as motivated almost exclusively by a lust for getting even.

Ironically, this premise about international terrorism, that it originates in envy of our privileged circumstances, is widely accepted across the often harsh socioeconomic lines within the United States itself, and is espoused on both sides of the political fence. It has been articulated by Americans in many different walks of life. As but one especially fierce illustration, the impassioned Ralph Peters, author of *New Glory: Expanding America's Global Supremacy*, responding to an interviewer's question about the Middle East's threat to the West, minced no words: "The populations of the Middle East blew it. They've failed. Thirteen hundred years of effort came down to an entire civilization that can't design and build an automobile. And thanks to the wonders of the media age, it's daily rubbed in their faces how badly they've failed . . . The terrorists don't want progress. They want revenge."

In the same interview, Peters succinctly summarized his— and our—belief that envy is the prime motivating factor in terrorism: "You've heard it before, but it's all too true. They do hate us for our success."

This is an appealing hypothesis. Somehow, it simultaneously addresses our vanity concerning our relative wealth and progress, and the uneasy guilt we sometimes feel over the same blessings when we reflect on the plight of many of our fellow human beings. In addition, the notion that terrorists "hate us for our success" allows us to view the enemy as completely irrational, and conforms to experiences some of us have had with envious acquaintances who became hostile and unreasonable when we acquired or achieved something positive in our personal lives.

But this viewpoint is oversimplified and misleading. It soothes us somewhat, with an extra boost to our well-known sentiments of being biggest and best, but it also abandons us in a dangerous position of ignorance regarding the actual roots and possible futures of terrorism. Seen through lenses that color terrorists uniformly green, all terrorist events are utterly straightforward, and their goal is achieved immediately and almost by definition. Terrorists hate and envy us, and therefore they desire to hurt us and to destroy our accomplishments. Thus motivated, they carry out terrorist acts, which are, by their nature, extremely destructive and hurtful.

And there you have it: the terrorists' vengeful objective is achieved instantly, every time. Terrorism always works, and, after the fact, there is nothing we can do about it.

But terrorism does *not* always work. The ambitions of its planners are more complex and far greater than a few finite moments of violent destructiveness that may (or may not) be motivated by jealousy and rage. A terrorist act may do horrible damage to fragile human bodies, or to our material achievements, or to the stability of our governmental systems. It may well gratify the jealousy and hatred of those who carried it out. Still—from the point of view of terrorists, terrorist organizations, and the history of terrorism—the plan does not work unless something else happens, too. Even a lethal terrorist plan is relatively unsuccessful *unless it affects our minds*. And the most successful attack, regardless of how much physical damage it does or fails to do, is the one that affects our minds most deeply and continues to affect them long after the knife's edge of grief has dulled a little, the demolished structures have been rebuilt, and the catastrophe itself has begun to recede into history.

The playing field is not the one we think it is. Terrorism's most important aim is not to damage bodies or our material accomplishments or our government, although these are certainly its most conspicuous effects. Rather, its most cherished ambition is to affect us psychologically, to instill a sense of helplessness in the minds of individual citizens, and to steal, in wholesale grabs, from our collective store of hopefulness. When completely successful on this psychological playing field, terrorism can evoke the skittishness and paranoia bred into our primordial ancestors, who were sorely challenged to survive as small and helpless creatures in surroundings made up mainly of physical threat. Though we live in a modern and allegedly sophisticated world, certain acts of terrorism flick a switch deep in the limbic system of the human brain, and suddenly—at least for a while—each of us feels as vulnerable and paranoid as a tiny colobus monkey at a leopard-ringed water hole.

And, as I will illustrate throughout the rest of this book, that is when terrorism really works—when it can blast an adequate number of its victims into helplessness and hopelessness, and into lasting animal-brain paranoia.

Successful terrorism uses fear to manipulate us. It is designed to get—and to keep—our frightened attention, even as we go about our day-to-day lives. The strategy is that of a playground bully who targets someone for random ambush beatings. Of course, the bully may get a charge out of watching his victim suffer physically, out of seeing the blood, hearing the sounds of fear and pain; but ultimately, it is a psychological game that he plays. What even the grade-school tyrant enjoys most is knowing that his victim feels helpless, and far too hopeless and isolated to turn to others for help. In this way, he gains influence over another person—keeps him in a state of fear and dread—not just at the time and place of the beatings, but day in and day out, perhaps for a very long time, and wherever his victim may go. Like schoolyard bullying, international terrorism uses abrupt physical force, but in both cases, the real payoff is lasting psychological power. Over and over, our history and our individual experience show us that the most effective bully, small or large, is the one who takes up residence in the mind.

When terrorist events are completely successful, people develop symptoms of helplessness and hopelessness. They almost instantly become suspicious of other human beings, including many of their own countrymen, and somewhat more gradually, their society or nation as a whole becomes suspicious of—and isolated from—the world at large. Terrorism that works does not merely murder people. As we shall see, it sets a trap of ancient origin in the minds of the living, one that claps shut quickly, while the survivors are still shell-shocked and oblivious, and one that may keep their psyches ensnared for years. Thus, a genuinely inspired terrorist leader measures his success less by counting physical casualties, and more accurately and triumphantly by how long his degrading emotional influence keeps its teeth sunk into the survivors.

For as long as people have lived in groups, terrorists have plotted to instill fear as the explosive punctuation to a message, one group to another. Typically, but not always, the would-be message-senders are members of a society that is far less powerful than the targeted group, and therefore less likely to be attended to when using a less bloody form of "communication." The boilerplate message of terrorism is the following: *If you* [the more powerful group] *fail to* [fill in the blank], *this* [the terrorist event] *is the kind of horror you can expect.* For example, *If you* [the United States] *fail to* [remove your influence from the Middle East], *this* [9/11] *is the kind of horror you can expect.*

Initially, the psychological trauma that preoccupies the targeted society is meant to make it impossible for the terrorists' communication to be ignored or forgotten. But in most cases, the fear greatly outshouts the message, and soon, only the fear remains. The terrorists' message, to which innocent people have been sacrificed, is lost. And the more the terrorists are later vilified within the targeted group, the more misrepresented and unclear their original point becomes. In the end, the specific message succumbs to the terror that was meant to convey it, and enduring psychological damage for its own sake becomes the entire prize for the terrorists.

That effective terrorism negatively influences the emotions and behaviors of whole countries is, at this point, all too clear to behavioral and medical scientists. In a white paper on terrorism, released in 2005 by an interdisciplinary task force of the American College of Neuropsychopharmacology, the psychiatrist Rachel Yehuda and the neurobiologist Steven Hyman refer to the "psyche of our nation" and emphasize that "the broad goals of terrorism are ultimately psychological, affecting entire populations well beyond the scope of physical destruction of terrorist acts." Resonating with the scientific findings are the concerns of policy analysts, the intelligence community, and military personnel who evaluate counterterrorism methods. The intelligence community and the military understand that, in the end, terrorism is a psychological strategy. They are well aware that, when they are working to minimize the damage caused by future terrorists, they must factor in that, alarmingly, the largest number of potential "casualties" may be among the living.

In fact, for the purposes of this book, I can usefully define terrorism as *violence committed with the primary goal of manipulating the minds of the surviving population.* In line with my definition, the Israeli scholar Boaz Ganor, executive director of the International Policy Institute for Counter-Terrorism, has written that "modern terrorism is a means of instilling in every individual the feeling that the next attack may have his or her name on it. Terrorism works to undermine the sense of security and to disrupt everyday life so as to harm the target country's ability to function . . . Thus, the target population becomes a tool in the hands of the terrorist in advancing the political agenda in the name of which the terrorism is perpetrated."

In the spring of 2001, less than five months before the 9/11 attacks, the military analyst Paul R. Pillar, a retired Army officer and a former deputy chief of the Counterterrorist Center at the Central Intelligence Agency, wrote hauntingly in his book *Terrorism and U.S. Foreign Policy* that the "objective [of counterterrorism] is partly a matter of not letting the fear of terrorism, or measures taken to avoid it, so disrupt the other business of the U.S. government or of U.S. citizens that it constitutes a victory of sorts for the terrorists."

And so, if we take the terrorists' point of view for a moment, we must regretfully conclude that the 9/11 attacks on the United States were successful. That day, destruction of the World Trade Center and a part of the Pentagon made for terrorism that *worked*. As we have already learned, according to all credible research reports, the majority of Americans immediately began to suffer from debilitating psychological symptoms—depression, disrupted sleep, difficulties paying attention at work or at school, intrusive thoughts about the event—and a few days later, nearly half of previously normal Americans were reporting at least one symptom of the clinical diagnosis of post-traumatic stress disorder: dissociative reactions, panic attacks, broken self-confidence. A full two months later, against all logic and factual information, 20 percent of ordinary Americans still sincerely believed it "likely" that they personally would be hurt or killed in a terrorist attack—that, as it were, the next attack had their name on it—and were accordingly scared to death. In other words, on the morning of September 11, 2001, fear took up residence in our minds.

And in the aftermath, fear, in various disguised forms, has shown very little willingness to leave. In 2004, applied health scientists at Indiana University published a "National Study of

Behavioral and Life Changes Since September 11." This study looked at *behaviors* rather than at psychological responses, as earlier reports had done, because behavioral changes (alterations in what people do) tend to be more enduring than reported emotional changes (alterations in what people consciously feel). "Therefore," they state, "investigation of behavioral changes as a result of the 9-11 attacks helps reveal individuals' relatively stable perceptions about terrorist threats and . . . the extent to which U.S. communities have developed a collective emotional orientation of fear." This "emotional orientation of fear," which remained after the initial terror was over, is revealed in our behavior—our enacted decisions, the things we actually do—and is a fearful state that can be conscious at times, but, at many other times, remains completely out of our conscious awareness. Often subterranean, this *tendency to fear* is unlikely to be something we could acknowledge or report, even if we were questioned. But our choices and our actions, when studied, can give us away.

The 2004 study looked at a nationally representative cross section of U.S. adults, and found that the 2001 events had inaugurated substantial and lasting fear-related changes in the lifestyles and behaviors of Americans. In this national investigation, 12 percent of the respondents reported that, after 9/11, they had improved the physical security of their homes, and 15 percent had begun to keep emergency stocks, such as food, gasoline, or cash. (If you did not store bottled water yourself—and the odds are decent that you did make some emergency preparations—ask your neighbors what they decided to do. Chances are better than one in seven that they purchased survivalist supplies.)

Twenty-three percent reported that, worrying about another attack, they had chosen one form of transportation over another. Twenty-four percent said that, as a direct result of 9/11, they had turned more to prayer, religion, or spirituality. Twenty-five percent, a full quarter of the people studied, had limited activities away from their homes. Eighty-six percent reported they had "regularly or very often" watched television in order to monitor a perceived threat of continuing terrorism. And 10 percent, one in ten people, had considered buying a weapon to defend themselves and their loved ones.

Of the people whose physical appearance might be construed by other Americans as Near Eastern or Middle Eastern, all voiced an increased perception of life-threatening danger.

Across the entire group of research subjects, other prominent lifestyle changes included the avoidance of crowded areas, expressions of antagonism toward Islamic cultures and individuals, and the exercise of increased caution regarding surroundings and people in general. Overall, using our behavior as a lens, the 2004 study provided a view of lasting underlying anxiety, suspiciousness, and isolation across the United States.

To illustrate—no matter how far you are located from lower Manhattan—if, at this very moment, an unexpected low-flying plane were to be heard in the sky outside your window, what might be one of your first associations? Here in my peaceful little New England community, I believe I know what mine would be.

In 2005, completing the picture begun by the 2004 report of behavioral changes in our domestic lives, Jeffrey Kleinberg published "On the Job After 9/11," the first reported study of the lasting effects of terrorism on the American workforce. Kleinberg, a New York City psychologist-psychotherapist, coined the term *worker's block*, and defined it as "a rapid emotional, attitudinal and relational disengagement from the job, that may not be classifiable as an illness, yet is powerful enough to create a personal and, if widespread, a corporate crisis." Worker's block involves not all, but three of the symptoms listed in the American Psychiatric Association's description of post-traumatic stress disorder: "markedly diminished interest or participation in significant activities," "feelings of detachment or estrangement from others," and the "sense of a foreshortened future" (which means, as the author extrapolates, that the individual no longer expects to have a career).

Kleinberg writes, "I soon discovered [after 9/11] that a sample of the people I was counseling had significantly changed their view of work and the workplace, rapidly disengaging from their jobs . . . Employees could not identify what was happening to them, and very few employers seemed to recognize the damage that had been done to their workforce."

Later in his report, Kleinberg graciously uses plain English to explain the experience of someone who suffers from worker's block: "The victim feels tired, and doesn't really care."

This succinct description may sound all too familiar to some of my readers. On the other hand, I suspect that, for many others, such depictions and all the statistics I have just provided do not feel personal at all. At this point, much of our "collective emotional orientation of fear" is substantially beneath our awareness. If questioned directly, many of us would sincerely protest that our lives, these years later, do not contain any thrumming undercurrent of anxiety resulting from terrorism. But in reality, the anxiety remains, requiring only small external triggers to propel it into the observable world of decision and behavior. Our choices and our actions, as a nation and as individuals, are still giving us away.

Like so many people, I believed that I personally had recovered from the shock of fear I had felt in September 2001, especially as the months and years began to pass with no further attacks within our borders. There were certain places on the globe I would have been nervous about traveling to, but my young daughter and I visited China and Mexico, and as time passed, I thought I was feeling almost as safe here in my own country as I had felt before. Besides, psychologists love statistics, and I knew the statistics on this particular subject were overwhelmingly on my side. With respect to fearing a terrorist attack in a shopping mall, for example, I knew it to be a fact that, since the odds of dying in an automobile accident each year are about 1 in 7,000, I was in hugely more danger driving my car to get to the mall than I was from potential terrorist bombs once I was inside. I had read the chastening *Washington Post* article by Michael Rothschild, professor emeritus at the University of Wisconsin's business school, who framed the issue this way: "There are more than 40,000 malls in this country, and each is open about 75 hours per week. If a person shopped for two hours each week and terrorists were able to destroy one mall per week, the odds of being at the wrong place at the wrong time would be approximately 1.5 million to 1." And, with friends, I had made the macabre joke that these odds lay somewhere between the odds of being killed by a dog (1 in 700,000) and those of being killed by debris from space (1 in 5 billion), two eventualities I had spent no time forfending against, or fearing.

But at the first small test, my faith in my own objectivity

about terrorism was revealed to be entirely misplaced. One evening in 2006, five years after the Trade Center attacks, my daughter and I were sharing some General Gau's chicken at a small table in the food court of a suburban shopping mall. We were very hungry and had just begun to eat when for no obvious reason, the central fire alarm for the mall went off. For about ten seconds, a heart-stopping metallic wail echoed against the skylights in the dome of the food court, until someone apparently got to the controls and made it stop. If the same thing had happened six years earlier, I would have startled at the sudden loud noise, just as I did in this case, but, in the absence of smoke or a panicked crowd, I would probably have attributed the fire alarm to a mistake or a prank of some kind, and when the racket had ended, I might well have continued to eat. Not this time, however. This time, in the year 2006, after the loud noise made us jump and then was silent, I looked at my daughter and she at me, and without having to voice our concern—without saying a word, in fact—we put down our forks, stood, and walked quickly to the closest exit. Neither of us said anything until we were already in the car and caught in the traffic jam that had formed because, ill at ease just like we were, everyone was trying to leave the mall at the same time.

As our car edged out of the parking lot onto the highway, I finally spoke. I said, "I'm not hungry anymore." She said, "I'm not, either," and then we both laughed. But there was little mirth in it.

There were no terrorists at the mall. The ten-second fire alarm was indeed a mistake, or an extraordinarily thoughtless prank, and the memory of the evening when I abandoned my Chinese food is far from traumatic to me. But the memory does

make me sad, for myself and for all of us, all of us who harbor so
much hidden dread, we whose minds house a lurking anxiety
that needs only a loud enough noise in a crowded enough place
to launch it into action. The memory does cause me to wonder
what else that same undercover paranoia is doing to my mind,
and to my life, as it waits there, quietly, to ambush my other
feelings—and how many of my behaviors and decisions? On a
personal level, I hate it that, albeit to only a tiny degree, the terrorists won, and apparently continue to win, *in my mind*. And
the psychologist in me feels her spirits weighed down by the
very math of it, by what can happen when we multiply the en-
trenched, camouflaged fear that resides in one person times
three hundred million people, especially when those three hundred million populate the most powerful nation on earth.

Of course, these observations tend to raise the objection *Yes,
but terrorist attacks always have this kind of effect, do they not?* The
notion of a "successful terrorist attack" implies that some attacks
are unsuccessful, but surely any country in which large numbers
of innocent people have been massacred by outsiders has reacted
psychologically more or less the same way the United States did
after 9/11. Is that not true?

As it turns out, the startling answer to this question is no.
Other countries have not always reacted with the same dramatic
and enduring emotions. Over the long human history of inter-
group violence, sometimes whole societies have been tripped
over into chronic fear and paranoid vigilance by terrorist activity, and sometimes they have not been altered in this way. Group
reactions to terrorism are surprisingly contextual. They vary
with place, timing, and other aspects of circumstance. Not all
nations behave the same way when terrorism strikes, and the

same nation may react differently at different points in its history.

Reactions to the 2005 bombings in London are a case in point. These terrorist attacks on the city's transportation system, the deadliest set of bombings in London since World War II, occurred on July 7. Between July 18 and July 20—less than two weeks later—researchers contacted a representative sample of adult Londoners by phone, and asked them about their levels of stress and about their intention to travel on tubes, trains, and buses, or into central London, once the transportation network had been returned to normal. Thirty-one percent of Londoners were suffering from "substantial stress," as assessed in the same way that the emotional impact of 9/11/2001 had been measured in the United States, and 32 percent said they intended to travel less by public transportation. But the majority of Londoners, more than two thirds of them, were not overstressed, and the researchers noted that there was "no evidence of a widespread desire for professional counseling." Journalists' descriptions of behavior tended to corroborate the scientific findings concerning the relative composure of the Londoners. For example, the BBC world affairs editor, John Simpson, observed, "Only three days after a savage series of bomb attacks in central London, half a million people turned out in the streets to applaud as the Queen, in an open car, led a parade of veterans down the Mall to Buckingham Palace." Simpson quipped that the huge crowd and the open car constituted a reasonably unruffled "Churchillian hand-signal to the bombers."

The only exception to the rule was that the attacks were followed by a disproportionate increase in distress among non-whites and Muslims, who faced a realistically heightened threat—not from terrorists, but from other Londoners.

Israeli society provides another significant illustration of relative equanimity under conditions of repeated and ongoing terrorism. In August 2003, an eye-opening study conducted by researchers at Tel Aviv University, "Exposure to Terrorism, Stress-Related Mental Health Symptoms, and Coping Behaviors Among a Nationally Representative Sample in Israel," was published in *The Journal of the American Medical Association*. Of the Israeli residents questioned, a full 16 percent had been directly exposed to a terrorist attack, and 37 percent had a family member or close friend who had been directly exposed. The study's conclusions were summarized as follows: "Considering the nature and length of the Israeli traumatic experience, the psychological impact may be considered moderate. Although the survey participants showed distress and lowered sense of safety, they did not develop high levels of psychiatric distress, which may be related to a habituation process and to coping mechanisms."

The Israeli psychologists Yechiel Klar, Dan Zakay, and Keren Sharvit have written, "The picture that emerges [in Israel] is one of realism." They note that the main and perhaps the only consideration that now tends to cause Israeli residents to alter their lives in a precautionary direction is a risk factor referred to as "perceived absolute vulnerability," in other words, the near presence of a realistic threat.

THE CONTRAST EFFECT FROM HELL

In a seeming paradox, despite the fact that terrorist assaults on the country of Israel have been ongoing, individual Israeli residents who are not realistically threatened by terrorism have managed to clear their heads of the terrorist's intended legacy of fear—and we, residing in the relative nonviolence of the United States, have so far not been able to do this. These cross-cultural findings assume an urgent real-life importance for American citizens, saddled as they are with lasting suspiciousness and needless levels of anxiety. What did the Tel Aviv University researchers mean when they wrote that the less drastic and more realistic reactions of the Israelis "may be related to a habituation process and to coping mechanisms"?

The psychological concept of *habituation* means, in basic terms, that a person can get used to almost anything if it goes on long enough. An example often given is that of the urban dweller who lives by an elevated train track. His visitors, their hands over their ears, ask him how he can stand to live with the bone-rattling noise of the trains that continually blast by his window. He answers, in all truthfulness, that he just does not notice them anymore.

Technically, habituation is a form of *learning* in which, with the repetition of a stimulus, there is a progressive lessening in the probability of a response. The "stimulus" can be a chemical in our bodies, or it can be something we perceive with our five senses, or a life circumstance, or anything else that would normally affect us. We can habituate to a drug that is used too often, needing more and more of it to get an effect. Our brains and our eyes can habituate to constantly viewed images, such that we do not "see" them anymore. And our emotional and behavioral responses can habituate to frequently experienced situations, making us less reactive to them. The learning involved in habituation is a fundamental process of creatures, from insects to humans, and does not require conscious motivation. It is normal, adaptive even. If we and our nervous systems never habituated, we would never be able to distinguish the changing and meaningful information in our world from the constant background "noise" of our surroundings. We would waste most of our energy on repetitious and irrelevant stimuli.

Another classic illustration of habituation, often used in psychology classes, involves a sleeping puppy. If you clap your hands loudly near a sleeping puppy, she will wake up, wag her tail, and begin to lick your fingers. If you wait for her to fall back to sleep, and clap again, she will wake once more. But by the third or fourth time you clap your hands during her sleep, she will remain asleep and unfazed. Your repeated attempts to wake her by clapping have habituated her to the very noise you were trying to use, which her brain has decided is no longer significant.

For the computer age, "banner blindness" is yet another example of this phenomenon, one that plagues online advertisers. If a Web page flashes you with the same commercial banner in exactly the same place on the screen every time you access the page, soon you will no longer "see" the banner, or be able to name the product or service it was designed to promote.

Just as we can acquire "banner blindness," and just as the city dweller became inured to the noise of all those trains, the Israelis—and people living in the British Isles, and many other populations around the world—after many terrorist attacks on them, have, to a fair degree, *habituated* even to terrorism. Habituation does not mean that terror fails to happen at the scenes of these horrific crimes, and sadly, it does not mean that innocent citizens in these societies do not die, or that families do not suffer the agonies of irreplaceable loss. But habituation does mean that most of the unaffected survivors are inoculated against the lasting over-the-top fear that terrorists attempt to instill as their highest priority. And because these habituated groups of people no longer react with sustained anxiety and draining fear-related behaviors, they are sometimes able to develop and use *coping mechanisms* that short-circuit the paranoia switch. As early as the first hours, days, and weeks after a disastrous event, they are able to speak realistically with one another about what has just happened to them, and to reject fearful rumors in favor of seeking helpful and accurate information. In societies that have experienced a number of terrorist events in their recent history, habituation creates a small cushion of mental space in which to take an all-important collective deep breath before reacting—an opportunity to consider the reality of the situation as thinking individuals, rather than as a shell-shocked group triggered by irrational myths and political hype.

In 2001, in the United States, we had almost no prior experience that might have modulated our emotions, no history that would have allowed us to "get used to" being assaulted within our borders. The full-scale international terrorist attacks on the World Trade Center and the Pentagon were the first within the continent, and what followed were our initial, completely *unhabituated* reactions to a profound and (from our point of view) unprecedented event—foreigners violently invading our homeland. The first cut is the deepest, and, as a nation, we felt impaled to the heart, and shell-shocked accordingly, by those first-ever foreign attacks on our continental soil. History had provided no cushion of mental space for us, and we were not allowed to take any collective deep breath before we reacted to the rumors, and to the ubiquitous spin-masters.

There was a moment, a fleeting one, when we did try to take that breath. Perhaps you remember? Our world seemed to turn sad, and also compassionate, for a few rarefied days after September 11, 2001. We called in to radio stations and wrote to our newspapers, in solidarity with one another. Strangers were kind, and drivers were courteous, as if something had just been put into extremely clear perspective. Grief-stricken musicians sang to us gently about how fragile we were. The faces of our celebrities looked human and prayerful, and our artists and our poets did what they could to give us the images and the words for what was happening to us. But the moment did not hold. With nothing to habituate us to the experience of being attacked in that way, the shock was too great, and soon, fear trumped the compassion and even the grief.

Beyond being simply unhabituated to terrorism, Americans were forced to deal with a psychological contrast effect that could not have been designed more exquisitely by the devil himself. Technically speaking, a *contrast effect* is the enhancement (or diminishment) of our experience of reality as a result of a previous experience or expectation. There to aid our bodies and our minds in making quick decisions based on past events, the contrast effect works on the perceptual level as well as on cognitive and social levels. In a psychology classroom, an easy demonstration of a *perceptual contrast effect* involves placing a student's left hand into hot water and her right hand into cold water, and then moving both of her hands to a bowl of lukewarm water. With both hands in the lukewarm water, she will report that her left hand now feels cold, and her right hand now feels hot. Probably no one in the class will be very surprised by this outcome. Upon just a little introspection, the contrast effect is a phenomenon that is familiar to most of us. As another illustration, this one on a cognitive/social and slightly more upsetting level, try looking at your face in the mirror after you have been viewing a great many made-up and airbrushed faces on television. How attractive do you look to yourself?

The contrast effect plays on our *expectations*, both perceptual (temperature, pain, and so on) and conceptual (beauty, safety, and so on). A good thing feels even better if our previous expectations have been negative, and vice versa: a bad thing will feel much worse if our expectations have been positive. The greater the difference between our expectations and what actually happens, the greater the contrast effect. This is why many medical professionals are taught (and why *all* of them should be taught) to provide patients with realistic predictions, if possible, regarding the amount of pain a surgical procedure is likely to cause. Anticipating the worst is no fun—and certainly, it is difficult to inform a patient, especially a child, that he is about to feel something bad—but even dread of the future is better than anticipating "This won't hurt a bit," only to find that a procedure has left one in considerable pain. When we do not expect pain, it feels substantially more agonizing when it comes, because our brains are wired for contrast effects, and some of these effects can be quite powerful.

On the early morning of September 11, 2001, we woke up in a country that we absolutely believed to be the safest on earth. We based our entire lives on that large and tacit expectation. To the north and south were our friendly neighbors. To the east and west, two wide, protective seas. Our military might was legendary, and whether or not all of us admitted the fact out loud, our slumber was deeper on account of that legend. And

then, on the morning of September 12, after a fitful sleep, we
woke up to remember that we were now in an alien-feeling
place where we could be annihilated by foreigners just because
we left our homes and went to work. At that moment, the contrast of it all felt nearly unbearable to us. We had been robbed of
more than our safety—we had been robbed of a part of our
identity.

Given the profound psychological shocks that ripped through
us at the time, the drama of our initial reaction to 9/11 is not
surprising. Rather, it is the present—and the future—that are
most at issue. These years later, we remain involved in a contest
between the American mind-set and a quiet but chronic "orientation of fear" installed by terrorism and its attendant wars. Will
we carry this orientation indefinitely into the future, or will we
be able to rise above it?

We know that terrorism has quite a track record. It has been
tripping the switch of fear at least since the first century BC,
when the Sicarii and the Zealots committed public assassinations
to terrorize the Roman rulers of ancient Palestine, and anyone
who supported them. Considered on such a formidable time-
scale, the American nation and the American personality are
brand-new, and almost untested. Will we be able to prevail
against the long-term psychological pressures of terrorism and
violence that have, for millennia, reduced countless other societies to hatred, rigidity, and infighting? In suspense of historic
proportion, the whole world is watching the land of the free,
the home of the brave, this grand experiment in human
liberty—and waiting for the answer to that very question.

Will we eventually return to our characteristic ideals and passions, the ones other nations have watched with interest and

hope since the eighteenth century? Or, contrary to our best nature, will we continue to be directed by subliminal fear and
paranoia? Will we regain our famous energy, and the humanistic
orientation that has at times brought us right out into the streets
to protest for our rights and for the humane treatment of others?
Or will the psychology of trauma and the politics of fear succeed
in dealing us the final injury—the permanent redirection of our
minds?

ORANGE IS FOREVER

One last small but crucial detail about how terrorism works is
this: after a nation—the United States, for example—fully un-
derstands that terrorism can happen within its borders, an
awareness of danger is established that has no reliable *safety signal*
to offset it. A psychological safety signal is any symbol or situation that indicates by its presence that a particular danger is temporarily absent. For a monkey in a sinister laboratory cage, a
green light that comes on only when electric shock is *not* being
used is a safety signal, one that provides the poor animal with
a brief mental vacation from the menace of shock. (In the
language of learning theory, when the green light—the safety
signal—is on, the probability of electric shock is zero.) If I am
standing on the sand, fifty feet back from the surf, the probability of meeting a great white shark is zero; therefore, dry land is
my reliable safety signal for shark attacks. If I am living in a war-
torn city, the announcement of a truce can be a reasonably reliable safety signal for bombs being dropped from the sky.

Safety signals are extremely valuable to us, and neuropsychologists think that a part of the brain, the infralimbic area of the prefrontal cortex, specifically codes newly found safety signals into memory, for our future use. They can help save our sanity, and our physical health as well. They say, "All clear," allowing us to take those deep breaths and to lower our pulse for a while, often quite literally. Safety signals cannot make danger feel neutral, but they can make it feel bearable, by providing us with occasional breaks in the ongoing stress of anticipation.

But terrorism has no reliable safety signal. As people have learned in Israel and in the British Isles, in Africa, in Indonesia, in South America, and from antiquity to the present, terrorism can happen anywhere, and at any time. Opportunities for our fellow human beings to use violent tactics can be lessened, but such chances will never be completely absent. Our own developing awareness of threat will know no sabbatical or endpoint. The danger of terrorism in the world will never again feel bearable in the innocent and old-fashioned way it used to, with "living in America" as our trusted safety signal. And so, as we are about to find in coming chapters, we must learn to make ourselves feel secure in a new way, one that we create psychologically. With our minds, we must insure that, even when it happens, terrorism simply does not work.

THREE

**THE DAY THEY CAPTURED
CAT STEVENS**

Paranoia is an antireligious mysticism based on the
feeling or perception that the world in general, and
others in particular, are against me or us. Reality is
perceived as hostile.

—SAM KEEN

Human beings are certainly not the only ones who feel
fear. The family dog is reacting in unmistakable terror when he
dives under the bed, or behind his mistress, with the first crash
of thunder. The limbic system of a laboratory rat lights up like a
holiday tree when its vigilant little eyes catch sight of another rat
looking aggressive on the other side of a Plexiglas wall. In fact,
evolutionary theorists tell us that the capacity for fear—"the gift
of fear," as threat assessment specialist Gavin de Becker calls it—
evolved in the minds of rodents and canines and people, and indeed all mammals, because, for instance, the gazelle who feels
fearful and inclined to flee at even the most equivocal sign of the

leopard's presence is likely to be blessed with a much longer life than the serenely trusting gazelle. In terms of survival on this planet full of dangers, fear is adaptive for everyone, from the tiny white-toothed shrew to the great blue whale.

However, though we humans are not unique in feeling fear, we do seem to be much better at it—more expressive, more elaborately prepared to meet threat, less able to put fear aside when threat is gone—than any other group of nature's creation. We are, in a sense, the masters of fear. Imaginative, and capable of easy leaps from one idea to the next, our big brains can make a case for being afraid out of almost anything—a shadow in the bedroom, our neighbor's house lights staying on all night, a curl of smoke in the distance, a hang-up call—and we want not just to be able to recognize threat, which is a reasonable and an adaptive ability for all creatures, but to control it, as well. From the first stone weapons we ever fashioned, to the most advanced and unsurvivable of our technological defenses, we have endeavored to control whatever frightens us. We have been, in fact, so superior at *fearing*, and at trying to control all that is fearsome in the world, that we ourselves have become the apocalyptic threat.

Where our reactions to potential danger are concerned, as with so many other emotional issues, survival calls on us to find and maintain a middle ground, because the far ends of the fear continuum lead to crazy behavior, and ultimately to self-destruction. If we did not fear at all, we would be like the calmly trusting gazelle, and most of us would not live to see puberty. We would be oblivious to predators, including the worst of the human ones. We would ignore all threats, take risks without a second thought, and be likely to meet death when we were children, perhaps simply by leaping off cliffs to see whether we could fly. The extreme of unshakable calm does not work. And the opposite extreme, intense fearfulness—which is the direction we, the masters of fear, are inclined to take—causes us to behave quite differently, but every bit as oddly. Excessive fear in a person, and certainly a chronic orientation of fear in a group of people, creates unpredictable psychological and social aberrations. Fear that is extremely great, or that hangs on indefinitely, with no safety signal in sight, can easily push our thoughts and our behavior over a line, and into that infamous territory where truth is stranger than fiction.

Having been a therapist for trauma survivors for many years, I thought I knew all about what fear could do to human beings, but September 22, 2004, seemed to be my day for learning still more about the irrational things that extreme fear can make us think and do, especially when a whole nation has been terrorized. I was driving my daughter to school on that sunny Wednesday morning in 2004, when someone announced on the radio that Yusuf Islam, formerly known as the singer Cat Stevens, was about to be deported from the United States, on grounds of national security.

"National security? *Cat Stevens?*" I asked out loud.

To my surprise, my daughter, then only twelve, said, "Cat Stevens? *The* Cat Stevens?"

The voice on the radio continued. It said that on the previous afternoon, Tuesday, September 21, United Airlines flight number 919, en route from London to Washington, had been diverted to Bangor, Maine, because the name of one of its passengers, Yusuf Islam, had been discovered on a government watch list. At Bangor International Airport, the closest airport at the time of this discovery, the plane had been met by agents from the FBI, and also from Immigration and Customs Enforcement, and Yusuf Islam had been removed. The London-to-Washington flight, with all the other passengers onboard, had then continued on its way to Dulles International Airport. A Homeland Security Department spokesperson confirmed that federal agents had interviewed a British citizen named Yusuf Islam, denied him entry into the United States "on national security grounds," and detained him. And on that day, Wednesday, September 22, 2004, Islam was to be put on the first available flight out of the country.

I think many of us heard about this event soon after it happened, and I am sure we had diverse reactions to it. If you are an American baby boomer, like me, it is a fair guess that you remembered a delicately handsome Cat Stevens from the 1960s and '70s, as the war in Vietnam was ending, sweetly singing songs like "Peace Train" and "Morning Has Broken" to your own newly awakening adult sensibilities. And perhaps you have a fuzzy memory of the fact that, in the late 1970s, the self-dubbed "pop star" abandoned his multimillion-dollar recording career and the stage name of Cat Stevens and took a Muslim name, having been persuaded by his orthodox teachers that the lifestyle of a wealthy celebrity was forbidden by Islamic law. But chances are that, like me, you were not aware of Yusuf Islam's more recent activities, until his 2004 grounding in Maine launched him back into the American consciousness for a while. For instance, not quite seven weeks after he was deported from the United States, Yusuf Islam was presented with the Man for Peace Award during the World Summit of Nobel Peace Laureates, held annually in Rome.

The Committee of Nobel Peace Laureates, in their formal

announcement of the 2004 winner, proclaimed that the musician had worked to "alleviate the suffering of thousands of children and their parents in countries of war and agony like Kosovo, Bosnia, Albania, Montenegro and Iraq, through Small Kindness, a humanitarian organization established by Yusuf Islam," and that he had dedicated himself to "promoting peace, reconciling people, and the condemnation of terrorism." Pointedly, the committee noted that Yusuf Islam had donated a generous portion of his royalties to the September 11th Fund, in the United States.

In the car that morning in 2004, remembering only a much younger songwriter named Cat Stevens, I muttered, "Oh no, here we go again. Now we're arresting the poets." And again to my surprise, and somewhat to my sadness, my young daughter already understood this sardonic remark about human history.

Still, the announcement of the detention itself was not what most wrenched my emotions. Mix-ups happen, especially when people are tense. (Immediately after the incident, Islam himself had remarked, "For God's sake, people make mistakes.") Presumably, there had been some confusion over a government watch list that had included a fairly common Muslim name. Rather, it was what the mistake triggered, the immediate outpouring of suspicion, hatred, and free-floating rage, that made me feel a little sick as I drove along my usual routes that morning and the radio station began to broadcast the near-unanimous reactions of the callers-in. No one suggested, "Maybe the authorities jumped to conclusions too quickly," because no one seemed to have the smallest problem believing that this former songwriter and current peace activist was a terrorist conspirator.

Instead, at the somber end, there were calls for capital punishment. On the more whimsical side, there were ethnic and religious jokes, quips that, little more than three years earlier, would not have been heard at all on most American radio stations, that now were confidently aired and followed by the sound of Americans howling with laughter. Most approvingly received was a song that seemed to center on the notion of being on an airplane and detecting body odor coming from the "dirty robes" of a dark stranger with a funny name. The composition, set to the tune of "Peace Train," both scanned and rhymed, and I was taken aback that someone could have come up with the lyrics so readily.

The instant verdict of guilty for someone named Yusuf Islam, and the belligerent little song, were disheartening reminders that, even after the passage of three years, the anxious paranoia and the anger from 2001 were not gone from our lives. To the contrary, certain aspects of the emotions had broadly generalized, had radiated outward to touch people and issues that many of us had once tolerated or even been charmed by. A sizable majority of Americans had been overstressed, even traumatized, by the terrorist events of 2001, and extreme fear can cause not only long-lasting emotional problems but also enduring changes in the physiology of the brain itself. As I listened to the suspicious voices and the derisive laughter on the radio, the trauma psychologist in me had this realization about the ideologically humane and well-intentioned people of the United States, and in subsequent months and years I would have many additional occasions to reflect on the same alarming neurological metaphor: *Our paranoia switch has been tripped.*

FEAR AND THE HUMAN BRAIN

To understand this metaphor—the image of a paranoia switch being tripped—we must consider how our neurological makeup processes the events of our lives and affects our behavior. When the brain processes ordinary (nontraumatic) experiences, the system works brilliantly, efficiently dividing and directing the wide and nearly endless river of information coming at us from our complex surroundings. When something—anything—happens to us, a part of the brain called the *amygdala* receives information from the physical senses, via another area of the brain called the *thalamus*, and attaches emotional significance to this input from the outside world. The amygdala then passes along its emotional "evaluation" to yet another part of the brain, the *hippocampus*. In accordance with the amygdala's "evaluation" of importance, the hippocampus is activated to the appropriate degree, and will organize the new sensory information from the world *according to its emotional priority*, and integrate it with already existing information about similar events.

This prioritized integration of new input with information from the past is extremely important. The process allows the so-called higher parts of the brain—the *cerebral cortex*—for example, to put together coherent, conscious memories for us, memories that we perceive as comprehensible wholes. And such "higher" memories—prioritized, integrated, and whole—have the crucial advantage of being dynamic, open to meaning-modification by future events and through language. They are alive, in the sense that they grow and mature. We can reflect upon such fully processed memories in our own minds, discuss them with other people, and reevaluate them if necessary.

Most of our remembered experiences are processed in this way, and end up as the phenomenon we experience subjectively as "memory," as in *I remember when Aunt Mary took me to the zoo to see the zebras.* Our conscious memories tend to be brimming with images that we can identify, with language, and with that most dynamic production of language, *tellable stories.* We can *tell* our memories to other people, and they can tell us theirs. And, over the years, the zoo memory will become even richer in its context, as the rememberer associates other people's stories with her or his own, and as the cerebral cortex compares notes with the past and receives additional emotionally prioritized input from future experiences with zoos, trips, zebras, aunts in general, and Mary in particular. Overall, our neurological sorting and integration process allows our memories to be informed, coherent, and meaningful, rather than chaotic and flooded with empty details.

But when new input from the world is radically stressful, and certainly in traumatic situations, the brain's recording process becomes overloaded, in a manner of speaking, and the otherwise brilliant system breaks down. Overwhelming emotional significance registered by the amygdala actually leads to a *decrease in hippocampal activation*, rather than the large increase in activation that one might expect, such that some of the traumatic input is not usefully organized by the hippocampus, or integrated with other memories. In other words, the "overloaded" hippocampus makes the tragic error of "neglecting" over-the-top input, as if it were insignificant, rather than of very high emotional priority. The result is that portions of traumatic memory are incompletely processed, and virtually ignored by the integrating and meaning-making ("higher") systems of the brain. These portions of memory are not stored as parts of a unified, intelligible whole, but, instead, as isolated sensory images and bodily sensations that are difficult for the person to associate with any particular time, situation, or story. When we are aware of the effects of these images and sensations (and often we are not aware), we experience them subjectively not as memory, but as undefined feelings, or mood changes that are difficult to shake. However, technically, they are nonintegrated pieces of a *memory*, the memory of an event so stressful that it "overloaded" the brain.

These memory fragments are *not* dynamic. They are "stuck"—unchanging, sealed off from being updated by subsequent, less traumatic experience, and inexpressible in language. They are wordless, placeless, and eternal, and long after the traumatic event itself has receded into the past, the neurological record of trauma—the paranoia switch that is now "stuck" in the brain—consists of anonymous, free-floating traces of strong emotion, image, and sensation that can "trigger" irrationally suspicious and inappropriately frightened reactions in the individual. These traces of memory cannot be modified by conscious thought, or by discussion with other people. This means that a person cannot deal rationally with his or her own paranoia switch, or debate it, or "uninstall" it by force of conscious will, or indeed, in most cases, even know it is there.

Worst of all, later in the person's life, in situations that are only vaguely similar to the original trauma—perhaps merely because events are startling or emotionally arousing—"stuck" traumatic memory traces are accessed more readily than are the more complete, less shrill memories that have been integrated and modified by the higher parts of the brain. Though unified and updated memories would be more judicious in the present, traumatic memories are more instantly accessible, neurologically speaking, and so trauma may be remembered at odd times, when there is no objective threat worthy of alarm. In reaction to relatively trivial stresses in the present, the person who has been overstressed in the past, and whose sensitive paranoia switch has been tripped, may truly *feel* that danger is imminent again, and behave accordingly.

The classic example of the inappropriate intrusion of traumatic memory fragments—the abrupt flipping of someone's paranoia switch—is the traumatized combat veteran who hears a car backfiring on the street where he is walking, and immediately dives to the pavement, just as if the sudden loud noise were gunfire from a sniper. For the moment, the former soldier believes he has heard a gun—he *feels* it—with as much certainty as you believe you are now reading or hearing this sentence, and all of his reflexes, thoughts, physiological reactions, and behaviors are those of a person who is trying to evade sniper fire. If one were to study his physiological status and that of a person who was actually being targeted by a gunman, there would be no difference.

His paranoia switch has been tripped, and in his mind, as he flattens his body to the sidewalk, he is not simply recalling the experience of combat. He is *there*. The staccato noise of the car backfiring was similar enough to the sound of gunshot that it accessed some of the free-floating memory traces of the powerful emotions, images, and sensations from the combat trauma that was endured in the past, and only minimally processed by his brain's overwhelmed hippocampus. And so, he is there. In the present, in less than the blink of an eye, his brain has transported him to a time long past, and to a distant war-ravaged place that was inestimably more dangerous than the sidewalk-lined street where he was just an instant before. He behaves accordingly: he immediately drops to the ground, to make himself less of a target to the sniper he absolutely "knows" is there.

To an objective person traveling along the same street at the same time, the former soldier might appear to be crazy. But he is not crazy. He is terrified, every bit as terrified as you or I would be if we knew we were about to be shot dead.

In this example, a gunfire-like noise set off ill-processed memory fragments "stuck" in the brain of a war survivor. (*Triggered them*, is the expression often used by trauma psychologists.) Anyone who has heard a car backfire can appreciate that, at least from a mildly paranoid frame of mind, the sound might be reminiscent of a shot. And most of us can understand that certain combat experiences might be permanently traumatizing. We feel a natural compassion for the former soldier and will likely suspend our tendency to be judgmental, even though his behavior sometimes looks extreme from our perspective. And, as our society learns more and more about combat post-traumatic stress disorder, once referred to as shell shock, its symptoms and its long-term psychological agonies, we are increasingly persuaded that PTSD should be studied further, and that our combat veterans should be provided with treatment.

The symptoms of PTSD include nightmares, exaggerated startle responses, and mental *flashbacks* to some aspect of the original trauma, such as the flashback our veteran suffered when he "heard" gunfire and reflexively dropped to the ground. The diagnosis of PTSD is correlated with a tragically high incidence of chronic anxiety, major depression, addiction, ulcers, heart disease, and, unsurprisingly, divorce and intractable relationship problems. Most of these painful symptoms and destructive life patterns result from the fact that, as I have just described, the brain reacts to traumatic experience differently from ordinary experience. Traumatic memories tend not to be adequately processed or made fully conscious. Instead, they remain in the brain as incoherent memory traces and sensations, constituting a cruel little hair trigger, a paranoia switch that, without some very good and informed therapy, may reside in the combat survivor's brain for the rest of his or her life.

Other people who suffer from PTSD, and all of its associated problems, are the survivors of grave childhood abuse and sexual violation. For the last twenty-five years, my therapy patients have been adults whose early pasts included such experiences, and I have detailed some of their stories in a previous book, *The Myth of Sanity*. There was the film producer, Julia, who was triggered into total memory loss for three days merely by the mention of the city where she had spent her tormented childhood. And I relate the case of Garrett, the house painter, who in childhood had witnessed the brutal murder of his younger brother, and who, as an adult, was thrown by even mild interpersonal stresses into extreme and destructive personality splits. And I describe—of all the professionals one might not expect—a psychiatrist who was abused in childhood by his violent mother, and who, as an adult, could be triggered into a fugue state (a condition of "walking amnesia") by a minor and completely unrelated argument with his wife. In all of these early abuse stories, just as with the combat survivor, strange behaviors are triggered later in life by vaguely similar events that activate inadequately processed traces of traumatic memory—by the tripping of a leftover paranoia switch in the brain. In more general terms, all of these cases illustrate the long-lasting and crazy-making effects of fear on the human mind, down to the actual gray matter.

YELLOW RIBBONS AND AMERICAN FLAGS

Although most of us exhibit moderately dissociative ("apart from ourselves") behaviors at times, few of us will ever forget where we are and drop to the pavement because of a sharp noise, or enter into a lengthy fugue state owing to a squabble with a spouse. This is because, happily, profound trauma re-peated over a protracted period of time is not usually part of our personal histories. Very few people have been in frontline com-bat, and relatively few of us have been near-lethally abused as children, or for that matter, repeatedly terrorized in any other way. However, unhappily, the paranoia switch that we have been discussing does not require life-threatening abuse or multiple traumas to be effectively installed. The formal psychological def-inition of a *traumatic event* is a circumstance that forces us to con-front our mortality—in other words, an event that emphatically raises the specter of death in our minds. And there are times—September 11, 2001, for example—when a single dramatic event, one that abruptly brings us face-to-face with the certainty of death, can overwhelm our brains, and leave us with the kind of inadequately processed memory traces that provoke inappro-priately fearful behaviors later on. After a single unusual event of this kind, we probably will not become amnesic for days at a time, nor will we dive to the ground each time a car backfires, but our lives will be affected in other, less conspicuous ways—because, in the aftermath, our very brains will be subtly and long-lastingly changed.

September 11, 2001, a day of terrors for which Americans had no inoculating precedent at all, injected our brains with countless overwhelming, free-floating images and vicarious sensations, and established a culture-wide paranoia switch just waiting to be touched off. Can you remember how you reacted on 9/11, in the minutes and hours when you began to understand what was happening in New York? If you are a parent, do you remember asking yourself in a panic, *Where are the children?*, even if you and your whole family were hundreds or thousands of miles from the attack? Do you recall the inventories, the mental lists you made of relatives, friends, and acquaintances who might conceivably have been in the Twin Towers, the haunting speculations about the people in your life who might possibly have been on airplanes that morning? The phone calls you made, and how alarmed you felt whenever, for any reason, you failed to get through? And then the strange emotional numbness that lasted for days—the unaccountable sense that all joy and vitality had crumbled along with the towers?

Later on, do you remember vaguely planning an escape route to . . . where? Or making sure your car was filled with gas, or wondering whether you should buy some bottled water and supplies for . . . what? Do you recall wondering, rehearsing even, what it would feel like to have a box cutter to your throat? Did you wonder what on earth people think about when they have courageously chosen to crash their own plane, or how they feel when they know their very last "I love you" has just been spoken into a cell phone?

There were so many other ruminations about what "it" must have felt like, so many horrible imaginings. Despite ourselves, we imagined—we *saw*—charred human corpses on elevator floors and severed limbs falling through the air. We imagined trying to escape down endless flights of stairs, with God knows what behind us, and stumbling over anonymous men, women, and children in absolute darkness. Though we were not all present on those Manhattan streets, many of us ran, and ran, and ran—in our minds—from the fire and the smoke and the thunderous noise of the catastrophe that could not possibly be real, but somehow was.

Perhaps worst of all, we imagined how it must feel to have a dearly loved parent, or brother or sister, or spouse—or child—in the morning, and by the afternoon, to have nothing but a photograph, a worn piece of paper, and to wander the city streets, desperately asking the same question over and over of all those other shell-shocked strangers.

Unintentionally, but repeatedly, the news reports taunted us with our most biologically prepared phobias, all of them at once—fear of heights, fear of fire, fear of confined spaces, fear of flying—and made hideously public our secret, primitive dread of sudden abandonment.

And then there were those iconic towers, those giant twin structures that seemed to be part of everyone's experience, even for those who had never so much as visited New York City. We saw twin towers in our mind's eye, again and again. We dreamed about twin towers, were haunted by our seemingly mysterious visions of them. In his review of the documentary film *WTC Uncut*, the journalist Matt Zoller Seitz wrote movingly of this phenomenon: "There was something primal, something univer-

sally appalling, in the image of those twin, featureless columns—
so smooth, so tall, so perfectly blank—gashed by planes, billow-
ing smoke and fire. The towers reached toward the sky; they
were . . . made (seemingly) permanent by movies, TV shows,
posters, postcards, snapshots; they were brought down in
102 minutes, and we were powerless to stop it."

In the same piece, Seitz wrote of the lasting damage he
thought might be done to our society by the searing of such an
image onto all of our minds. He was right, even righter than he
perhaps knew. This iconic symbol and myriad other traces of
traumatic memory insinuated themselves into our gray matter,
invisibly, anonymously, and beneath our awareness. Very soon
after, the triggers that could evoke these memory bits generalized from the original, direct ones—crashing planes and explosions, and the faces of our fellow human beings in shock—to
include events, words, things, and especially *people* only circum-
stantially or symbolically related: airports, shopping malls, subways, cell phones, shoes, Iraqis, Syrians, Libyans, Iranians,
"national security," Middle Eastern faces, "vital interests,"
WMD, DOD, CIA, CNN, Al Jazeera, Afghanistan, Islam, men
in robes, "evildoers," "preemptive war," our troops, yellow ribbons, American flags, firefighters, fundamentalists, Arabs, Muslims,
Muslim names, and on and on, virtually ad infinitum—until we
were swimming in a veritable aquarium of traumatic memory
triggers. At this point, for many Americans, a fire alarm in a
public place, or words such as *jihad* or *fatwa* in a newspaper
headline—or a Muslim name in a broadcast—can access "stuck"
memories established in a time of great fear, in a way similar to
the backfiring of a car, or holiday fireworks, or the call of a trop-
ical bird in a pet store can do to the brain of a shell-shocked vet-

eran of jungle combat. And like the war veteran, we tend to feel and behave accordingly. We do not dive to the pavement—nothing so conspicuous as all that—rather, we feel and behave in ways that are somewhat more anxious and suspicious than our usual reactions, with no conscious awareness of what is happening to us, or why.

When someone named Yusuf Islam was deported in 2004, the people whose belligerent comments I heard on American radio did not instantly *think* that Cat Stevens was a threat to them and their country. Rather, they instantly *felt* that he was a threat—a compelling misfiled memory fragment born of fear, and not a rational *thought* at all. To put it succinctly, their paranoia switch had been tripped.

On the surface, each of us deals with fear in his or her own way. I have my strategies when I am afraid, characteristic coping mechanisms, both conscious and unconscious, and you have your own. Yet in general, across all groups and coast to coast, our more fundamental reactions to that traumatic event were universal, because they resulted from our common neurological "wiring." To varying degrees, the emotional systems of our brains were overwhelmed, and our minds became more cluttered than we knew with unprocessed fragments of emotion, image, and fear-laden sensation. These chaotic shards of memory soon started to be triggered, and to ambush us at unpredictable times, altering our feelings, our moods, and our behaviors. Like the shell-shocked combat veteran whom we regard in a special light, all of us deserve to be considered with compassion and concern, even now. A few years ago, fear took up residence in our very brains, and, worse, most of us were, and continue to be unaware of our inner vulnerability.

Moreover, as we are about to see in the next chapter, fear is contagious. In a sense, when the brain's emotional system is stressed, it *broadcasts* fearfulness. A single riveting reminder that death is inevitable—that, indeed, death may occur at any moment—blasts the individual's limbic system with stressful input, and from there, the neurological effects of extreme stress flash like an electric current through increasingly large numbers of human brains, one to the next. And in this regard, research has shown, intriguingly, that some forms of traumatic stress are even more psychologically toxic than others. Most overwhelming of all are traumatic experiences caused not by accident (unintended explosions or car crashes) or by "acts of God" (earthquakes, volcanoes, etc.), but rather by the deliberate acts of other people, acts such as assault, violent abduction, rape—or terrorism. It would seem that, for whatever reason, we are hardwired to be most fearful of harm when it threatens to occur maliciously, at the hands of our fellow human beings, and this special variety of fear is the most contagious of all.

To explain how terror that has invaded some brains can be invisibly "caught" by other brains, I begin the next chapter with a 1995 case from my trauma practice, in which a little girl becomes possessed of a debilitating fear that, by rights, belongs to her well-meaning mother. As we continue this discussion of how fear has changed all of our brains since 2001, I turn back now to 1995, and the revealing story of Leena and Wynn.

FOUR   FEARING AS ONE

> We cannot live only for ourselves. A thousand fibers
> connect us with our fellow men.
>
> —HERMAN MELVILLE

They say when you're dying, your whole life flashes in front of your eyes," Leena told me at her first therapy session. "But it isn't true, at least not for me. I didn't see pictures. I don't think I saw anything, period. I just kept screaming, 'Make it stop! Make it stop!' and that's all I really remember. Then I woke up in the hospital, and—surprise, surprise—I wasn't dead."

Leena said this as if, even in the middle of her terror, she had been cheated out of something important. That she felt she had been cheated, or stolen from, perhaps by life itself, was an impression I often got from her, though she never said so explicitly. My impression came more from the downwardly traveling tone of her voice, a disappointed and self-deprecating inflection she used in describing many of her experiences, not just the grisly one.

In the way of many trauma survivors, Leena possessed few coherent memories of the event that had left her with scars over the entire left side of her body, from foot to ear. In therapy, to gain a clearer insight into what had actually happened, we made do with the reports witnesses had given, and with accounts she had clipped from newspapers just after the incident. Yellowed, and worn from Leena's many rereadings of them, the twelve-year-old newspaper articles told a hair-raising story.

On that afternoon, newly married Leena, then only twenty-four years old, was driving home after visiting her mother, who lived about half an hour away from Leena's house, by a newly constructed divided highway. The day was rainy and foggy, so she had set out early for her drive, while there was still daylight.

"Before the accident—before that day—I was always a blasé kind of a person. I never really worried, if you can believe it—I mean, looking at me now. Okay, whatever—that's sort of how I felt about things. Normally, I wouldn't have thought twice about a drive like that after dark, but the fog was really terrible. I guess I shouldn't have done it at all. But, like I said, I just wasn't much of a worrier then."

Leena was right. Looking at her by the time I met her, a dozen years after that day, no one would have concluded that she was blasé. At the age of thirty-six, a face already lined with worry made her appear at least fifty, and the honey-blonde hair that framed her sad expression was turning gray. Most of the physical scars had eventually been smoothed by cosmetic surger-ies, but the marks on her frame of mind were still very much in evidence. When seated, she crossed her arms and legs defensively, and her eye contact with me tended to be fleeting, especially when we discussed the long-ago accident.

According to the local newspapers, on the afternoon of the accident, she drove away from her mother's house, pulled onto the new highway, and had driven only about two miles when the eighteen-wheeler sideswiped her Toyota.

Her memory of the crash itself was sketchy:

"I was driving in the far right lane, and I was going slowly—it was so foggy—and then, all of a sudden, the big truck on my left side started to pull right, into my lane. Into me! I screamed and I screamed. I think I tried to blow my horn. I'm not sure. It happened so *fast*. At some point, I do remember thinking, 'This is really going to happen to me. I'm going to die.' And then I was in the hospital. I don't remember getting there . . . I mean, I don't remember the rescue. That part's all a blank."

According to eyewitness accounts, the truck had slammed Leena's car into the guardrail on the right, but had maintained its speed, dragging Leena inside her crushed vehicle some two hundred yards, before the truck driver apparently noticed there was a problem. After what seemed an eternity to the onlookers, the truck pulled away to the left, and eventually came to a stop. What was left of Leena's mangled car came to rest in a ditch beyond the flattened guardrail. The ambulances, and the Jaws of Life, arrived quickly.

At trial, the truck driver claimed he had neither seen nor heard Leena's car as he collided with it. Finally becoming concerned about a scraping sound he thought he heard to the right side of his rig, he pulled left, and only then had he realized what was making the noise. The court awarded Leena all of her medical and court costs, plus $1.5 million for anguish and suffering. Her physical recovery was long, and involved a number of surgical procedures over the subsequent two years. When I met her, she still had only limited use of one of her legs. And she was left with a facial neuralgia, a severe pain that sometimes radiated from her face into her left arm, a condition the doctors said was likely to be permanent.

"The pain always reminds me that death can come at any time," she told me, solemnly and sadly, as if she were the bearer of some long-pondered wisdom. Unfortunately, to me, she sounded not so much old and wise as like a relatively young person who was still debilitatingly shell-shocked.

Soon after the crash, just after she got out of the hospital, she began to suffer from an "anxiety disorder," as she expressed it. She fell into constant worry and jumpiness, recurrent nightmares, and panic attacks. The panic attacks occurred not just in the car, though those episodes were the worst, but also in public places, such as theaters and malls. For a long while, she could not go shopping or even to see a movie. She did not enter therapy during the first years of her "anxiety disorder," because she felt strongly that, if she was ever going to get completely over the accident, she needed to "tough things out."

As most lives do, Leena's life had its dark and its bright spots, and the very brightest part of Leena's life at the time was her new husband. A calm and well-grounded young man ("the salt of the earth," as she put it), he would always take her home when a panic attack started, and stay there beside her until it subsided, patiently trying to comfort her.

"He did all the shopping, and when we felt like it, he'd bring home some videos," said Leena. "He was super. He really was."

And then, two years after the accident, and just as she was recovering from the last of her surgeries, a "miracle" happened for Leena, to use one of her own expressions again. She got pregnant, and nine months later, gave birth to a healthy little girl whom she named Wynn.

I asked her about her child's interesting name. With a radiant smile on a face that was too often unsmiling, she explained that her most important mission in life was to make certain that her miraculous daughter became a happy person.

"My life got screwed up—I'm so passive and helpless, like a tiny little mouse—but Wynn was so beautiful and *alive*, from the instant she was born. Really, she was. And, just by chance, I found this little baby-name book that listed W-Y-N-N as a girl's name. Get it? *Wynn* sounds like *win*—the direct opposite of *lose*."

Leena made it very clear that becoming a mother had been thrilling for her. Nonetheless, frustratingly, her near constant anxiety had continued to plague her even after Wynn arrived. My psychologically minded readers may already be wondering about the intensity and longevity of Leena's reaction to a car crash, albeit a horrible one, especially since her social and financial supports were so good. And indeed, as she and I discovered during her therapy, Leena's continuing problem was caused not just by the original trauma, but by another factor as well—her secret, needling doubt that the accident had truly been an accident, a simple matter of being in the wrong place at the wrong time. Instead, in her heart of hearts, she feared the crash had been intentional. Despite herself, she was deeply and unremittingly suspicious of the stranger who had driven the truck, and this mild paranoia had kept her anxiety fueled and running for more than a decade. At her third session with me, she confessed that she often thought about the truck driver, and that the thoughts of him terrified her.

"He was a total stranger—still is, really. The only time I ever even saw him was in court. But I can see his face in my mind's eye, just like one of my best friends'. No, to be honest, I can imagine *his* face even better than other people's. It's creepy, makes me feel like clawing my eyes out. His blue eyes, and that crew cut! Only, in my mind, it's not normal blue eyes. It's more like the devil's eyes. Evil. Do you think he dragged me along like that on purpose, Dr. Stout? I know it sounds crazy, but I don't have anybody else to ask. They'd think I was out of my mind."

We discussed this question over and over, during a number of sessions, and in the end, Leena always decided that the driver of the truck had caused a terrible accident, but had not possessed any intention of doing so. The accident was an accident. This was Leena's intellectual conclusion (the correct one, I feel certain), but the *feeling* that she had been specially targeted by the blond, blue-eyed devil-man with a crew cut, mauled on purpose by the paradoxically terrifying image in her mind's eye, never completely left her in peace. Her altered version of the truck driver was nearly always the central figure in the frequent nightmares that woke her in the middle of the night.

The torment of having this kind of satanic image in one's head would have brought many other people into therapy years before, but Leena had not sought treatment on account of her own misery. At last, she had decided to enter therapy only when her little daughter, Wynn, began to show unmistakable signs of anxiety and panic.

"There's no reason for it!" Leena grieved. "Nothing bad ever happened to her. And I never even told her much about my accident. When she got old enough to ask about my leg, I just told her I'd *had* an accident, and that was all I said. As God is my witness, I never said any other thing than that!"

When Leena first came to see me, in 1995, Wynn was nine years old. Her fourth-grade teacher had been trying to impress on Leena that her little daughter was having a painful struggle with anxiety, a problem that other teachers had noticed in the past. Wynn was finding it more and more difficult to participate in classroom activities. Worse, she was withdrawing from her friends. Leena had not been at all receptive to the notion that Wynn was an anxious child, and had told herself, and the teacher, that her daughter was simply passing through a very "shy" stage.

But then, in February of that school year, Leena had received an emergency phone call from the principal's office. In the school cafeteria, Wynn had just suffered what the teacher later reported she would certainly have called a "panic attack," if Wynn had been an adult rather than a nine-year-old. When all the other children had gotten up from lunch, thrown away their trash, and raucously begun to leave the cafeteria for their play period, Wynn had stayed quietly seated at her table, seemingly staring at nothing. The teacher had approached her gently, to remind her that it was time to leave.

After a long moment, Wynn had whispered to her teacher, "I can't."

Following her instincts, the teacher had sat down with the child for a full twenty minutes, talking to her soothingly. Finally, with the support of her teacher's arm, Wynn had been cautiously guided to the office, where Leena had been called and given the news.

To say that Leena was alarmed by the incident would be a large understatement. Rather, she had "completely freaked out," to use yet another of her own expressions, and had spent the next week in a frantic search for the most highly qualified professionals to evaluate and help her daughter. The pediatric practice in Boston that she and her husband had finally chosen used a very thorough team approach. Various members of the team had evaluated Wynn and interviewed her teacher and her parents. Leena made her first appointment to see me just after the team had given its report, which included a treatment plan for Wynn, along with the strong recommendation that Leena herself enter therapy, and a footnote of concern that Leena had never been advised to seek out therapy after her near fatal accident.

Having been a trauma psychologist for so long, and having listened to so many adults with crippling anxiety give their accounts of childhood abuse and other atrocities, I anticipated that the report would painfully contradict Leena's assertion that "nothing bad" had never happened to her daughter. I fully expected to read that the professionals on the team—a developmental psychologist, a child psychiatrist, two pediatricians, and a social worker—had discovered some evidence or symptoms of traumatic experiences in the child's life. If this was so, I wondered uneasily whether my new patient might be responsible, or perhaps her husband. Was I about to learn that Wynn's father was not really the "salt of the earth" at all, but a very different sort of person?

When I read the report, I was taken aback, and immensely

relieved, to find that it contained no such findings. The pediatric team had concluded that Leena and her husband behaved in a warm and loving manner toward Wynn, both in public and in private, and that their parenting skills were "good to very good." There was no sign that Wynn had been abused or otherwise traumatized in her young life, at home, at school, or anywhere else. Her father did not suffer unduly from anxiety, nor did he have "any other discernible psychopathology." In the team's opinion, the mother's "premorbid status," meaning Leena's psychological condition prior to the traumatic accident, had been good. In other words, before the crash, she had not been a highly anxious person, nor had she suffered from any other mental illness. And the family as a whole, at the time of Wynn's anxiety episode at school, had not been undergoing any particular crisis or special stress.

Wynn's developmental level was normal, and her physical health was excellent. There were no indications of any neurological problem that might help to explain her serious anxiety. Furthermore, despite her fearfulness during classroom activities, Wynn's scholastic performance was above average, as was her tested IQ.

In summary, apart from her sometimes paralyzing anxiety, *there was nothing wrong with Wynn* or with Wynn's life. A thorough process of elimination established that the only factor that could have caused Wynn's anxiety was her mother's anxiety, and this was the final judgment of the expert team. Surprised as the professionals were to have discovered no underlying psychopathology, and no hint of trauma in this child's history, they had found none. And in the final analysis, they had found no other life circumstance likely to result in such severe anxiety.

The team concluded that Wynn's anxiety disorder had been directly caused by *Leena's* anxiety disorder. And Leena's anxiety disorder was one aspect of a post-traumatic stress disorder caused by a near fatal accident that had occurred long before Wynn was conceived.

But how could this be?

Can anxiety somehow be contagious? Can a mind communicate directly with another mind? As it turns out, neuroscientists are beginning to understand that, through an astonishing neurological process called *limbic resonance*, the answer to both of these questions is yes.

THE BRAIN AND THE DAWN OF EMOTION

In 1878, a French neurologist named Paul Broca pointed out to the scientific community that, just under the cerebral cortex of the mammalian brain (the "advanced" part of the brain), there were several very intriguing structures of gray matter. Since these structures formed a kind of border around the underlying brain stem (the more "primitive" part of the brain), Broca assigned them the designation *limbic lobe*, from the Latin word *limbus*, which denotes a surrounding or a ring. Today, we refer to this part of the brain, between the cortex and the brain stem, as the *limbic system*, and we know that it is composed of several crucial brain structures, including the hypothalamus (the bridge between the nervous and endocrine systems) and two structures I mentioned in my earlier explanation of traumatic memory: the hippocampus and the amygdala. Together, these limbic structures enable a wide range of fundamental mental activities, such as the processing of our experiences with other people (*social cognition*), the appraisal of the *meaning* of our experiences, and—perhaps most important of all—the regulation of our *emotions*.

In addition to regulating our emotions, the limbic system is a major arbiter of which of our *memories* will be consciously accessible and which ones will not be, and has a powerful influence on our *goal-directed actions* and the *motivations* that induce us to take action in the first place. And, with its central location between the "advanced" (rational) and the "primitive" (instinctive) parts of the brain, and its wealth of neural pathways leading to and from both, the limbic system may well be the area of the brain that is most in charge of integrating the brain as a whole.

Neuroscientists still debate exactly where the limbic system begins and ends in the brain, anatomically speaking. However, whatever their location in the brain's physical geography, the various structures of the limbic system all use the same specific neurotransmitters (brain chemicals), are highly interconnected, and function in complementary ways. Moreover, all limbic structures appear to have developed for the same evolutionary reason: many eons ago, the elaboration of these brain structures bestowed a big adaptive advantage on the small, newly evolved mammals who, without some form of mental superiority, might easily have lapsed into extinction via the teeth and claws of the then physically dominant nonmammals.

The limbic system as a whole is a kind of central command post for certain functions that are necessary to the very survival of mammals, including humans. It discriminates between experiences and situations that "feel" good (*Approach this!*) and those that "feel" bad (*Avoid that!*), and enables the brain's record of experience (i.e., long-term memory) to reflect this emotional—

and often life-preserving—distinction. It is the limbic system that fuels important behaviors requiring emotional motivation, such as the play behavior of our young, which is a critical ingredient in learning and social development, and our adult inclination to nurture our vulnerable children, even when they are no longer infants. The emotions themselves—playful elation, family affection, rage, hatred, sadness, sympathy, joy—arrived on earth for the first time with the mammals, because the mammalian brain came with a watershed structural change—the fully developed limbic system.

Reptiles do not have evolved limbic systems, and they do not possess emotions as we know them. Their young do not play with one another. And those rare adult reptiles whose fixed action patterns include protecting their newborn offspring behave as if the little ones were strangers—meaning, in some cases, that they are food items—as soon as they leave babyhood. Somewhere in the misty evolutionary past, nature drew a radical line between the nonmammals and the mammals. On the mammalian side of the line (our side), there are beings who exhibit a colorful and intensely motivating characteristic never before seen on the planet, *the ability to experience real emotions*—sorrow and playfulness, greed and generosity, revulsion and love.

Emotion—all that warm-blooded, volatile, illogical affect—created transcendent possibilities for future living things, including humanity's very best chance for a final destiny as lofty as world peace directed by moral ideas. Peace on earth may seem quite an abstraction to us, discouragingly distant at best. Nonetheless, the possibility does exist, because out of that prehistoric mammalian emotionality—the clustering of little rodents, the loyalty of canines, the nurturing tendencies of ancient primate mothers—eventually grew the new and highly charged affective phenomenon of *human conscience.*

In 2005, in *The Sociopath Next Door,* I proposed the first psychological definition of conscience, as distinct from the long-standing theological and psychoanalytic ideas, noting that the field of psychology had been strangely silent concerning the meaning of that concept. According to my definition, conscience is a compelling feeling of obligation that is always based in our proclivity to bond with others, our (nearly) universal ability to love. Once we understand the true nature of conscience, we can appreciate that it is precisely our capacity to form emotional attachments that gives rise to moral character—and that the inability of an individual to form emotional bonds underlies a tragic distortion of the human psyche, sociopathy, characterized by the *absence* of conscience.

Conscience is not an intellectual code of right conduct, although it can motivate our adherence to such a code, and it is not Freud's punitive superego per se. Rather, conscience is an emotion. And when living beings evolved to possess an emotional faculty, including a tendency to form emotion-sealed attachments with one another, any ultimate future became conceivable, even a morally directed and nonviolent world. In fact, because of the extraordinary moral possibilities they open for us, the highly developed emotional functions of the human brain may, in the end, prove more earthshaking than our celebrated capacity to think rationally.

Ironically, the above is said in the carefully rational language of science. More poetic ways of making the same observation might be the related tenets found in many of the world's sacred texts—for example, the elegant biblical explanation that states simply, "God is love."

And all this came to the planet via Broca's little lobe of gray matter. For almost half a century now, intrigued scientists have been directly examining this tucked-away corner of the brain, by manipulating it in various ways. The earliest (and most callous) of these studies involved animals, often primates, from whom central structures of the limbic system were experimentally ablated (surgically removed). The early experimenters found that the removal of important parts of the limbic system caused animals to lose all *ludic interest* (tendency to be playful), and to cease, utterly, all nurturing behavior toward their young. In the 1970s and '80s, far less horrifying studies were done. Scientists discovered that direct (and non–tissue-damaging) electrical stimulation of limbic sectors evoked visceral sensations and emotions in human beings. The emotions and emotional phenomena awakened by stimulation of the human limbic system included anxiety, fear, intense feelings of familiarity, and vivid hallucinations that felt like dreams or memories. In 2004, again using human volunteers, neuroscientists at the Brain Imaging Research Division of Wayne State University School of Medicine found that, employing functional magnetic resonance imaging (brain scans) in real time, they could detect activation of the limbic system while subjects viewed emotionally "aversive" pictures, and that there was substantially less limbic activation when subjects looked instead at emotionally "neutral" images.

It is crucial to understand that, when researchers use electrical stimulation to induce an emotional response in humans, the particular response aroused is not related to the exact spot in the limbic system where the electrode is placed. *There is no direct relationship between a particular emotional response and the activation of specific groups of brain cells.* Instead, the person's particular response to the surge of "pure" emotion evoked by stimulation of the limbic system is determined by her personality and her ongoing issues and concerns. For an illustration of this important distinction, we can return to my therapy patient, Leena. Leena did not possess a limbic system that contained a little knot of neurons devoted to making her terrified of truck drivers. What she possessed was a limbic system that had been generally overwhelmed by a traumatic accident, and the resulting flood of fear, released by her limbic system, occurred in the defining context of knowing that a blue-eyed truck driver with a crew cut had caused the accident. The situation in which Leena found herself shaped her particular reaction, the one she could tell me about in words, after Leena's limbic system had thrown open the floodgates of pure, indescribable fear.

LIMBIC RESONANCE

At present, we understand that the limbic system plays a dominant role in regulating our feelings, the accessibility of our memories, our motivations to act, our ability to make meaning of our experiences, and even our consciences. But, for our discussion here, the most fascinating finding of all is that it has a *perceptual* job to do, a function that makes the limbic lobe similar to the areas of the brain that support hearing and vision. With our ears, their input processed through the brain's auditory system, we can perceive the acoustic energy transmitted by pressure waves in the air (sound). With our eyes, their input given definition by the occipital cortex, we can perceive reflected wavelengths of electromagnetic radiation (light). And with information from any or all of our senses, processed through the limbic system, we can perceive *the internal state of another human being*—her or his physiological and emotional status—to which we would otherwise be "blind." The neurological process that enables us to sense the emotions of other people is called *limbic resonance*.

Not only does the limbic system allow us to perceive the emotions of others—and others to sense our own emotional whereabouts—it functions, also, to align our emotions with those of the people around us, and vice versa. Our limbic systems receive and transmit emotional information in wordless neurological "conversations," and within these exchanges, work hard to bring different brains together into similar emotional states.

According to three eminent psychiatrists who have written extensively about this process, Thomas Lewis, Fari Amini, and Richard Lannon, limbic resonance is "a symphony of mutual exchange and internal adaptation whereby two mammals become attuned to each other's inner states." As I suggested in the first chapter, limbic resonance is the attribute of the brain that makes it more exciting or more teary-eyed to watch a movie with another person, rather than alone. And the existence of limbic resonance helps to explain the ancient and ubiquitous notion that the eyes are the windows of the soul. Lewis, Amini, and Lannon write, "Eye contact, although it occurs over a gap of yards, is not a metaphor. When we meet the gaze of another, two nervous systems achieve a palpable and intimate apposition."

How does all this happen? If the auditory part of the brain tunes into our ears' sensitivity to mechanical radiant energy, so that we perceive sound, what does the limbic system tune into, so that we perceive emotion? Scientists are still not sure. The neuropsychoanalyst Allan Schore, who studies how the infant brain first learns to regulate its emotions, refers to the interactive "transfer of affect" between one limbic system and another as *intersubjectivity*. He hypothesizes that, to achieve intersubjectivity, the limbic system is processing nonverbal expressions "embedded in facial and prosodic stimuli." *Prosodic*, in this case, refers to the rhythmic and intonational aspects of speech, and the facial and prosodic cues Schore proposes are the other person's facial expressions and tone of voice. For example, one person's frightened facial expression can be perceived by another person's amygdala in seventeen to thirty-three milliseconds, which is considerably less time than it takes to speak the word *scared*. Additional "embedded" messages might be derived from posture, olfactory stimuli, apparent physiological changes (sweating, flushing, slowed or accelerated breathing, etc.), tempo of movement, and subtle but detectable indications on the part of the other person that a particular action is about to be taken.

Ross Buck, a professor of communication sciences at the University of Connecticut, refers to limbic resonance as "spontaneous emotional communication." According to him, this form of communication "employs species-specific expressive displays in the sender [displays discussed above as facial expressions, physiological changes, and so on] that, given attention, activate emotional preattunements and are directly perceived by the receiver." This means that our brains were built to receive emotional signs from other human beings instantly and without effort—no intermediate processes—just as those same brains are "wired" to see light-reflecting objects in our eyes' line of vision, right away, and whether or not we are trying to perceive them. We can choose *not* to focus our attention on the objects before our eyes, perhaps not even to notice them at all, but our brains cannot *not* perceive them.

Because facial and prosodic displays contain embedded nonverbal messages that go back and forth effortlessly between people, Buck too describes emotional communication as "a conversation between limbic systems," and writes that this limbic exchange is "a biologically-based communication system that involves individual organisms directly with one another: the individuals in spontaneous communication constitute literally a biological unit."

Sensing the emotions of another human being is, then, a little like smelling a rose. When we perceive a flower's fragrance, there is no thinking (cognition) involved, and we are not aware of how, neurologically, we are going about perceiving the scent. With complete immediacy, we simply smell the rose. And, as it turns out, we can sense and resonate to the emotions of another person, and vice versa, every bit as directly. We tend to conceive of ourselves as communicating with other people via language, a form of sending messages back and forth that is conspicuous, conscious, and safely voluntary. But language is only a part of what is going on, in some cases only a small part, and one that can (and often does) distract us from the deeper meaning of our interpersonal encounters. Words can communicate information, ideas, overt commands, and the questions we are willing to make public. Limbic systems, on the other hand, can mutually communicate our emotional and physiological experience, and they communicate this complex information completely without words—inconspicuously, outside of our awareness, and whether or not we are trying to express anything. And so, for a moment, sometimes for much longer, we are joined together with another person or a group of people as "literally a biological unit." It is difficult to imagine a more genuine form of communication.

Limbic resonance, this direct neurological tie between and among creatures, operates constantly and powerfully, in us and also in animals less sophisticated than we. As an illustration of its influence in the "lower" primates, a study published in 1998 reported that the cerebrospinal fluid of grown bonnet macaques who had been raised by macaque mothers exposed postpartum to stress (highly inconsistent foraging conditions, in this case) contained the elevated levels of certain neurochemicals one might have expected in primates who had undergone stress themselves. Apparently, where the emotional systems of their brains were concerned, each of the macaque mother-baby dyads had, for a time, been a "biological unit."

We now know that, for a human infant, being part of this kind of "biological unit" with an adult caregiver is nearly as necessary to survival as nutrition and shelter. It is exclusively through limbic resonance with a consistently attending adult that an infant learns how to regulate emotions neurologically, to experience and modulate his or her own brand-new limbic activity. Mother's limbic system "speaks" to baby's, and vice versa, in vital and ever more complex lessons in how to feel, when to feel it, and how to calm the feeling before it becomes overwhelming to the inexperienced infant brain. An empathic, limbically "talented" human parent, responding at just the right moments—in a language of movement, expression, and tone that predates humankind itself—is an inestimable blessing for a child. Even given sufficient food and shelter, a human baby who is completely deprived of physical and emotional contact with a caregiver (as in a sterile orphanage or an abusive household) will, at best, live the rest of his or her life in the bitter isolation of profound attachment disorder, and at worst, simply perish in infancy.

Watch any normal human baby, and you will see that, whenever mother is close enough, the child monitors her facial expressions continuously. And when, in the experimenter's laboratory, mother is asked to freeze her face for a moment, providing no emotional display, her baby will become distressed and quickly begin to cry. It is apparently one of the human child's most primal instincts that, to be whole, he needs limbic resonance with his mother almost as much as he needs milk.

To a lesser extent, the adult limbic system, too, can be reformed through emotional union with another individual's brain. People who are effective at helping adults heal emotionally—that is to say, good therapists—rely heavily on the recalibration of emotion that can occur through limbic resonance, whether or not they are aware of this feature of their work. Many contemporary psychotherapists have pondered the similarities between a gifted healer and, to use Allan Schore's description, "the psychobiologically attuned intuitive caregiver of a securely attached child." And interestingly, nearly a century ago, though he could have known nothing of the neurology of limbic resonance, Sigmund Freud told his students that the effective therapist must "turn his own unconscious like a receptive organ towards the transmitting unconscious of the patient," so that the therapist's unconscious could "reconstruct" the patient's.

With a nod to the common Middle English derivation of both the verb *to affect* (as in, to influence) and the psychological term *affect* (emotion), we can say with certainty that we human beings *affect* each other continuously and powerfully, whether or not we are aware of our impact. This neuropsychological "influence process" is the underlying reason many mental health professionals, during the post-9/11 crisis, urged us to be mindful that our children's emotional reactions would closely correspond to our own. Also, limbic resonance is one of the many reasons that personality, and especially character, should be primary considerations in choosing our leadership. For good or for ill, a high-profile leader can have a radiating emotional influence on large numbers of people. And the phenomenon of the masses resonating to a single individual's emotions has expanded immeasurably in an era when even the subtlest aspects of a leader's facial expressions, movements, and voice can be televised repeatedly, to millions.

WYNN WINS

Limbic resonance bonds us emotionally. It can guide us, and sometimes it can heal us. It is the lovers' rapture as they gaze into each other's eyes, and the gentleness in a new mother's touch. Unfortunately, the radiant energy of limbic resonance also inspirits the angry mob, the destructiveness of group hysteria—and the demoralizing anxiety we have felt, as one, since

9/11. And limbic resonance means that even the most lovingly protected of our children can "catch" our worst fears.

My patient Leena had always been fiercely determined to protect her little daughter, Wynn, from the debilitating anxiety instilled in her by a traumatizing car crash that had occurred nearly three years before Wynn was born. So, of course, Leena had not communicated her fear explicitly to Wynn, had never passed along her story in words. But without Leena's willing it to happen, or even knowing it was so, her brain had communicated her emotions nonverbally, directly to her daughter's brain. To restate the blunt conclusion of the professionals involved in the case, *Leena's anxiety disorder had directly caused Wynn's anxiety disorder.*

Much to her credit, Leena broke through her understandable desire to reject this conclusion; she sought help for her daughter, and also for herself. The child psychologist chosen by the team to work with Wynn was seasoned, calm, and very gentle, and, in my opinion, took just the right approach with her nine-year-old charge. She described herself to Wynn as someone who taught kids about feelings, and explained that she wanted Wynn to learn some good new "skills" to deal with her "anxiety attacks" (as Wynn now called them herself), and eventually to make them go away. She explained, in realistic and nonpathological terms, what anxiety was and how it worked. She did *not* say to Wynn that she had a "disorder," or that she was in "treatment," or that she was a "patient."

Wynn had not suffered any seriously traumatizing life experience to cause her anxious reactions. Her anxiety was "pure," or "free-floating," meaning it was not anchored to any particular situation, thing, horrible event, or type of person (as in, sexual contact, or reptiles, or earthquakes—or blond, blue-eyed truck drivers). Thankfully, there were no intricate dynamics of trauma, paranoia, or dread swirling through Wynn's mind, and so her problem could be addressed directly, using education about anxiety in general, and specific anti-anxiety techniques. Wynn's psychologist taught her some self-hypnotic skills, which children tend to learn readily, and which decrease tension in the muscles, increase parasympathetic (resting) tone in the nervous system, and restore a sense of personal control over internal events. She taught Wynn how to recognize the bodily signs of her anxiety while they were still at manageable levels, before they had a chance to become overwhelming. And, since even nine-year-olds function better with conscious coping than they do with shadowy family secrets, Wynn and her new "emotions teacher" (with her mother's blessing) discussed her mother's anxiety, where it actually came from, what her mother "looked like" when she was anxious, and what Wynn could do—and especially what she could *not* do—about her mother's difficulties.

Wynn and her "emotions teacher" met weekly for a year. I have no way of knowing whether the child and the soothing, characteristically serene clinician were able to establish a limbic resonance powerful enough to be healing for young Wynn, but I think that, in the context of all the other successful work they did together, this kind of spontaneous bond could well have been formed. In any case, after a year, Wynn was completely free of panic attacks, and the school reported that, at recess, she could often be found playing and laughing with her friends.

Leena and I had a different type of work to do, lengthier and more difficult. But she agreed to do it, "for Wynn." Unlike her daughter's, Leena's tetanizing emotions were not apropos of

nothing and free-floating. Instead, Leena's fears were rigidly af-
fixed, riveted with rusty neurological nails, to a horrible event—
and, worse, to a specific type of human being. Cruelly, trauma
had rigged her brain with little hard-to-avoid trip wires of
paranoia. These could set off a panic attack by any discussion
of, thought about, or loose association to the blue-eyed truck
driver she still irrationally suspected of having crushed her on
purpose—or by truck drivers in general, or sometimes merely
by encountering a stranger with dramatically blue eyes or short
blond hair.

The distinction between Wynn's problem and Leena's is similar to the difference between feeling very anxious walking
down a strange street after dark, and feeling very anxious walking down a strange street after dark *because* you are half-sure
there are deranged murderers hiding in the bushes. In the first
situation, learning facts about the neighborhood, and walking
along the street safely a few more times, can reduce your anxiety. If you are experiencing the second type of emotion (which
is now full-fledged fear), no amount of experience with reality
can lessen your misery. This is because your fear is now focused
on a certain category of people (murderers who hide in bushes),
and your continuing thoughts about them (your paranoia) will
effectively block any calming influence or factual information
that additional experience could otherwise provide. Even if you
take the same walk again and again, you will keep imagining
those hidden killers—every shadow will further convince you
they are there—and this pulse-racing preoccupation will prevent
you from taking in any new information about how safe the
street actually is (or is not). As for the murderers—without literally beating the bushes, you will never know for sure whether or

not they contain homicidal maniacs. In fact, any imagined source of fear that is mysterious, or hidden from direct scrutiny, can easily remain in the mind's eye, appearing ever more terrifying, for a lifetime.

Yearning to impose order on chaos, our gray matter energetically resists the world's gray matters. Especially in fear-evoking situations, the brain is prepared to categorize unfamiliar people as either completely good or utterly bad. And when fear is evoked by an overwhelming real-life event, as it was in Leena's case, attributing the terror to an enigmatic source—especially an "utterly bad" human one—wraps a convoluted illusion around the already tangled predicament of a brain altered by psychological trauma. Leena's recovery was not a simple matter. In therapy, before we could begin to deal with the lasting neuropsychological effects of the trauma she had endured, we needed to address her mind's subsequent conversion of an ordinary truck driver into a shadowy figure who was scheming and evil.

After Leena became comfortable with me, she agreed to be hypnotized. Carefully, over a number of sessions, I induced and deepened her trances and taught her how to use the hypnotic state to visualize people from her past much more clearly than was possible when she was awake. We began with positive memories: the face of a dear old friend she had not seen in several years, her husband's joyful expression the day Wynn was born. Next, she practiced her visualizations with neutral memories, such as the facial expressions of people she knew less well, which was somewhat more difficult. Finally, we used Leena's trances to help her visualize, in as much detail as possible, the face of the driver who had caused her accident. Since she had seen him only in a courtroom, I asked her to use her mind's eye to "see" him in that setting. Hypnosis is quite calming, so she was able to recall her nemesis without becoming painfully anxious, as she certainly would have done in a waking state. As she "looked," I asked her to describe him aloud—the clothing he had worn to court, his mouth, his crew cut, the blue of his eyes—until, gradually, in a deeply relaxed state, she could look at his face and into his eyes, and "see" him not as a fantasy figure, but as an ordinary human being. I asked her to "look" many times, using part of many sessions in this way. After three months, even when she was not hypnotized and not in my office, Leena could calmly and realistically picture the person who had driven the truck, and the nightmares that featured him had completely stopped.

With the sticky seal of paranoia at last removed from her thoughts, our even more difficult task could begin: Leena and I spent the next two and a half years working toward her recovery from the chronic debilities of post-traumatic stress disorder. Her therapy was long, but I am happy to say that, by the time it ended, she no longer suffered from the crippling anxiety caused by having been nearly crushed to death.

THE TRILLION-DOLLAR QUESTION

In the weeks and months immediately after September 11, 2001, our entire nation was suffering from a similar crippling anxiety. As a group, we were nearly consumed by our fears. With little previous habituating experience, one in five Americans believed they would "likely" be hurt or killed in a terrorist bombing, and one in four were convinced they would be hurt or killed by an act of bioterrorism. Strong evidence informs us that life-threatening heart rhythms more than doubled in Americans who had heart conditions. And the mechanisms of limbic resonance made our fears highly contagious. Terror radiated neurologically, and, in a flash, the entire population reacted as if it were a single "biological unit" facing the nearness of death. Though most of us were far from the scene, we experienced the desperate emotions of trying to escape from a lung-blistering inferno. More than empathy, we *felt* the grief of losing a loved one into a mountain of smoldering debris. And, as if we were but a single dreamer, we had common recurrent visions of those iconic flaming towers.

As one thinker—as a national mind—we planned for survival, and pondered being confined to our basements. Predictably, the ugly sealing glue of paranoia began to seep into our thoughts, and soon we would be making disastrous group decisions with the potential to haunt us for decades, affecting our futures and the lives of our children.

We were scared to death, three hundred million of us, reacting as one.

At this point, I would like to ask you, my reader—with all this in mind—to imagine an outlandish scenario. Imagine that you, personally, are the leader in charge of millions of such people. Having just been profoundly injured at the hands of inscrutable human beings from a distant part of the world, your citizens are traumatized and paranoid. The resonance of their fear is almost palpable. They turn to you, en masse. And, prepared to trust your answer implicitly—to cling to it, even—they ask you the following question:

What should we do now?

I believe that, as you looked out on all of your vulnerable followers, your desire to help them would be huge. You would
earnestly want to bring them some comfort and peace, so that
they could recover, protect themselves, and rebuild. And, you
may be wondering, would not anyone in such a rare and influential position wish to do that?

But there are those who have different desires. Beginning in
the next chapter, I will discuss what some powerful leaders have
actually done in the aftermath of trauma. We have completed
the first phase of our "group therapy," and looked squarely and
realistically at what befell us, psychologically and neurologically,
as a result of 9/11. The next phase in returning to our right state
of mind is learning to recognize who is—and who is not—a retraumatizing merchant of fear.

FIVE

THE LIMBIC WARS

> Voice or no voice, the people can always be brought
> to the bidding of the leaders. That is easy. All you
> have to do is to tell them they are being attacked,
> and denounce the pacifists for lack of patriotism
> and exposing the country to danger. It works the
> same in any country.
>
> —HERMANN GÖRING

As Leena's trauma therapist, what would I have done if the driver who caused her tragic accident had indeed been a calculating sadist who acted intentionally—a "terrorist," if you will? My answer is that I would have conducted her therapy in almost the same way. She and I would have needed to acknowledge that he had hurt her deliberately, and I might have helped her think through the resulting legal implications. But after she had faced this horrifying aspect of the incident, I would have encouraged her, as I did in the "nonsadist" situation, to learn to visualize him as a real human being, as clearly and calmly as possible. I would have done this so that we could proceed with the rest of her trauma therapy, and so that she could courageously and *realistically* evaluate any legal options that might protect her and other people from this dangerous perpetrator in the future.

I was the authority to whom Leena had turned for help, and for me to focus our sessions on her horror and outrage would have been cruel, whether or not the truck driver had acted intentionally. With only a few words, I could have enhanced her already evident tendency to see him as larger than life and unmeetably powerful, and if encouraged, the paranoid image of a larger-than-life perpetrator will soon take up permanent residence in the human mind. If I had centered our work on the man who caused the accident (villain or not), I could have postponed indefinitely Leena's recovery from the post-traumatic stress disorder brought on by the accident itself. Also, by galvanizing her fears concerning this larger-than-life figure, rather than working with her to reduce them, I would almost certainly have instilled in her an unnecessary dependency on therapy, and on me. Her "treatment," and her allegiance to me as the "authority" in this matter, likely would have lasted much longer than two and a half years. And, had her nemesis been an actual sadist, Leena would have been in danger the entire time, since she would have developed no rational plan to protect herself from a life-sized and altogether human enemy.

An individual predicament like Leena's is almost identically mirrored by the plight of traumatized groups and nations, except that, for nations, high-level political considerations also come into play. In the wake of trauma, these political matters involve an inherent conflict of interest between a nation and its leaders. If a leader chooses to focus the group's attention on the terrifying "others"—if he or she pounds the paranoia switch installed by trauma—the group's fear level is likely to remain over the top for a long time, and, whether or not he is competent, the leader's perceived authority will hold. If, on the other hand, a leader chooses to address the actual needs of the people at such a time—self-protection, recovery, rebuilding—the group's paranoia and fears will diminish more rapidly, and people will soon feel more competent themselves, and less desperately dependent on the leader's authority. In other words, after a traumatic event, a moral leader must voluntarily relinquish an uncommonly good opportunity to cast his political power in psychological stone. And, in contrast, to secure his political advantage, a less moral leader may well choose to wage a veiled emotional war against his own people.

We know there is nothing new under the sun, and covert limbic warfare is no exception. It is a technique that has been used throughout the ages to consolidate and maintain power over populations made vulnerable by traumatic events. In sixteenth-century Italy, Niccolò Machiavelli, whose very name has come to signify ruthless deceit, proposed that politics was above moral law. In his treatise *The Prince*, he described pragmatically amoral strategies, including the revival of preexisting fears in the population, that he believed would help absolute rulers maintain strong central governments. Quoted by political theorists for nearly five centuries, one of Machiavelli's more famous claims is "It is much more secure to be feared than to be loved." And Napoléon I of France, widely regarded as the greatest commander who ever lived, is credited with the chilling precept "Men are moved by two levers only: fear and self-interest."

Though the United States is a relatively young nation, we have already been through a number of our own limbic wars, destructive struggles with small cadres of people who have tried to enlarge their projects or their influence by using whatever our collective anxieties happened to be at the time. Let us examine some of these homegrown examples, beginning with the farcical first year and a half of the most notorious fear-mongering group in U.S. history, the Ku Klux Klan.

The KKK was born in the nineteenth century, from the still unfathomed national trauma of the Civil War. Incubated in the shell-shocked American South, the Klan launched itself into full-fledged existence easily, one might even say accidentally. In the small town of Pulaski, Tennessee, six college students, all former Confederate officers—James Crowe, Calvin Jones, John Kennedy, John Lester, Frank McCord, and Richard Reed—met and decided to form a fraternity, by which they meant a kind of social club, with the goal of relieving some of their peacetime boredom. Between Christmas Eve of 1865 and the summer of 1866, the young fraternity members amused themselves with noisy after-dark pranks in their small community, putting on odd-looking disguises, mounting horses, and galloping point-lessly around town. To their ignorant surprise, the students dis-covered that their nightly stunts were invoking real fear in Pulaski, especially among those of the residents who, but a short time before, had been slaves. Sadly—and fatefully—many of these frightened people looked at the riders in their strange homemade costumes and believed they were seeing the mounted spirits of the dead. Pleased by the unexpected effect of their horseplay, and their own sudden power, the six began to recruit among the like-minded in the town, and soon, their fra-ternity enjoyed a considerable swelling of its membership. The townspeople were only too willing to take out the destruction, humiliation, and anxiety of a losing nation on their newly emancipated fellow citizens. Similar fraternities began to form in other towns, and in April 1867, a central meeting was held to establish rules and an organizational structure.

The name chosen by the original Pulaski group, "Ku Klux Klan," was intended to lend an air of mystery to their association and is a slurred amalgam of the Greek word *kuklos*, meaning wheel, circle, or band, and the English word *clan*, denoting a group of people with common concerns, or descended from a common ancestor. Thus christened by a band of six "brothers" who had signed on merely to amuse themselves using the post-war fears of their neighbors, the KKK began its ultimate expansion into the largest authoritarian hate group in the history of the United States.

THE JAPANESE ARE COMING

The birth of the Klan illustrates all too clearly that, after group trauma, large-scale social changes can be inaugurated, intentionally or not, by a handful of scaremongers who play to the anger and paranoia of a vulnerable population. As these changes occur, the power of the few is enhanced, and the truth—that this power is founded in the larger group's stress—can be all but invisible, especially to those who are being manipulated. Such a pattern of events is reasonably easy to identify in retrospect, and nearly impossible to see while it is happening.

With the advantage of long retrospect, we can recognize another American example of this pattern in the years just after December 7, 1941, a date that is comparable in its psychosocial effects to September 11, 2001. We now understand that the history of this example, the relocation and internment of nearly 120,000 Japanese-Americans, is essentially a story of racism. As the nineteenth century closed, there were only about three thousand Japanese people living in the United States. Then, in 1898, Hawaii became a U.S. territory, and all people living there were suddenly at liberty to move to the mainland. By 1908, the Japanese population in the continental United States had risen by more than 135,000, and most of these new residents had settled on the West Coast. California politicians and labor leaders pushed to restrict immigration into the state, and in 1924, the United States prohibited Japanese immigration altogether. Japanese individuals who were in the United States already, the Issei, were forever barred from American citizenship, but those of their children who were born here, the Nisei, were declared to be citizens already.

Even in such a hostile atmosphere, the Japanese immigrants prospered, and by the time World War II had begun its ugly rumblings in Europe, many were farm or business owners, or successful fishermen who owned their own boats. Of course, their very success brought complaints from older farm and business interests and from the established fishing industry on the West Coast. The white citizens screamed to their local politicians, and the politicians complained to Washington. Still, if nothing else had happened, this situation might have remained merely the ancient and sad human story of unfamiliar-looking newcomers against "natives"—both sides claiming the higher moral ground—in a competition over territory and finite resources.

But on December 7, 1941, something else did happen, and

the shock of the sneak attack on American soil at Pearl Harbor
wired the national paranoia switch with a vengeance. Even those
of us not old enough to remember directly have heard the stories about how terrified Americans from California to New
York prepared for the Japanese bombers to appear again, this
time perhaps over their very backyards. Ramping up the already
disastrous level of fear, President Franklin D. Roosevelt's Secretary of the Navy, Frank Knox, announced that he attributed the
Pearl Harbor attack to "the most effective fifth column work
that's come out of this war, except in Norway." Entirely without
evidence to support his claims, he made a number of specific al-
legations, including a statement that local Japanese fishing boats
had furnished information to the enemy about the locations of
U.S. warships. In all likelihood, Secretary Knox was aware that
the local military's lack of preparedness had contributed to the
success of the attack far more than had any sort of espionage,
and pointed his finger at a mysterious "fifth column" in an attempt to prevent the U.S. Navy from losing too much face. He
used this fear tactic despite the U.S. military's own conclusion
that a large-scale invasion of the mainland was well beyond the
capacity of the Japanese military, with or without spies.

Knox's move to scapegoat the Japanese-Americans opened
the dam for a flood of sensationalistic newspaper stories, each
more provocative and unsubstantiated than the last. This media
campaign both reflected and amplified Americans' fears of saboteurs within their borders, and of an imminent full-bore attack
from without. Those who dared to voice their skepticism about
such threats were labeled naive at best, and at worst, abettors of
sabotage.

On February 13, 1942, the *Los Angeles Times* ran an article entitled "The Fifth Column on the Coast," written by the influential journalist Walter Lippmann (who later in his career would, ironically, popularize the word *stereotype*). In this piece, Lippmann stated unequivocally, "It is the fact that communication takes place between the enemy at sea and enemy agents on land." Lippmann somehow construed the fact that no raid on the mainland had occurred to be evidence that, at that very moment, a plan for a colossal future attack sat on the Japanese-American drawing board.

Though Japanese submarines were indeed patrolling off the California coast, neither the Federal Communications Commission nor the Federal Bureau of Investigation could find any evidence of contact between the vessels and the people who lived along the shore. Nonetheless, the psychological tenor of the American press was terrifying. As but a few indications of the media influence most of us have read about in our history books, the following headlines appeared in the *Los Angeles Times* between December 1941 and February 1942:

SUICIDE REVEALS SPY RING HERE
Japanese Doctor Who Killed Self After Arrest
Called Espionage Chief
[December 19, 1941]

WHAT TO DO IN CASE OF POISON GAS ATTACKS
[December 19, 1941]

JAP SUBS RAID CALIFORNIA SHIPS
Two Steamers Under Fire
[December 21, 1941]

JAPAN PICTURED AS A NATION OF SPIES
Veteran Far Eastern Correspondent Tells About Mentality
of Our Enemies in Orient
[December 23, 1941]

REPRESENTATIVE FORD WANTS ALL COAST JAPS IN CAMPS
[January 22, 1942]

NEW WEST COAST RAIDS FEARED
Unidentified Flares and Blinker Lights Ashore Worry Naval Officials
[January 25, 1942]

OLSON SAYS WAR MAY HIT STATE
Shift of Combat to California Possible, Governor Declares
[January 26, 1942]

THE QUESTION OF JAPANESE-AMERICANS
Perhaps the most difficult and delicate question that confronts our
powers that be is the handling—the safe and proper treatment—of our
American-born Japanese, our Japanese-American citizens by the
accident of birth. But who are Japanese nevertheless? A viper is
nonetheless a viper wherever the egg is hatched.
[W. H. Anderson, February 2, 1942]

CALIFORNIANS SEEK MORE ALIEN CURBS
Washington and Oregon Members of Congress Join in Plea for
Expansion of Program
[February 3, 1942]

AMERICAN JAPS REMOVAL URGED
Internment of All Dual Citizens Asked by County Defense Council
[February 3, 1942]

VENTURA COUNTY URGES REMOVAL OF ALL JAPANESE
Supervisor Demands Drastic Measures in Seeking Evacuation
from Coast Area
[February 4, 1942]

LOYAL JAPS MUST AID FIGHT AGAINST SABOTAGE,
SAYS OLSON
Governor Asserts Action Will Be Taken to Curb Spy and
Fifth Columnist Activities
[February 5, 1942]

JAPANESE HERE SENT VITAL DATA TO TOKYO
American-Born Nipponese Had Powerful Radios to Transmit Messages,
[Chairman] Dies [of the House Un-American Activities Committee]
Will Disclose
[February 6, 1942]

ARMY ORDERS SABOTAGE ALERT HERE
Warning Issued for All California
City Placed on Air Raid Alert
[February 7, 1942]

MILITARY CONTROL OF ALIENS ADVOCATED
Defense Council Wants Army and Navy to Police Foreigners
in Combat Zones
[February 12, 1942]

LINCOLN WOULD INTERN JAPS

[Los Angeles Mayor] Bowron Says Civil War President Would Move
Aliens If in Office Today
[February 13, 1942]

DANGER IN DELAYING JAP REMOVAL CITED

Congress Warned Speed Necessary to Prevent Widespread Sabotage
Attempts on West Coast
[February 14, 1942]

There were steadily increasing pressures on President Roosevelt to isolate the Japanese-Americans—and, into the bargain, a forty-year-old history of racial and economic tensions—and on February 19, 1942, he signed the infamous Executive Order 9066. This order removed nearly 120,000 Japanese-Americans from their homes and forced them to move into ten remote relocation centers in Arizona, Arkansas, California, Colorado, Idaho, Utah, and Wyoming. All 120,000 people, 62 percent of them U.S. citizens, were summarily stripped of their civil rights, which rights FDR proclaimed to be "contingent." According to the historian Greg Robinson, of George Mason University, the political pressures on FDR were so great that he deliberately permitted himself to be misled in his decision-making by biased counsel and bad information. He signed the relocation order despite the fact that the more reliable reports available to him, including one by J. Edgar Hoover, had unanimously concluded that there was no "fifth column," and no national security threat of any other kind from the Japanese-American community. Three years later, the Supreme Court upheld the constitutionality of the detentions, arguing that it was acceptable for the government to curtail the civil rights of a racial group in times of "pressing public necessity."

After being forced behind the barbed wire that surrounded the "War Relocation Camps," many of the people wrenched from their homes did not again see the world outside the fences until the end of World War II. And more than forty years passed before the formerly interned Japanese-Americans received an official apology, signed by President Ronald Reagan in 1988, on behalf of the U.S. government. This federal legislation included the opinion that the relocation of the Japanese-Americans had been motivated by "war hysteria" after the surprise attack on Pearl Harbor. History has now judged Manzanar, and the rest of the Japanese-American internment program, to be, as the attorney Christopher Brauchli has expressed it, the story of "a dignified group of people being treated in an undignified way by a government rendered constitutionally insensate by fear."

THE RUSSIANS ARE COMING

The day after Pearl Harbor was bombed, and within an hour of a stirring address by President Roosevelt, Congress declared that a state of war existed between the United States and Japan. Three days after that, with no dissenting vote, Congress acknowledged a war with Germany and Italy, and on that same historic occasion, revoked an article of the Selective Service Act that prohibited the use of our armed forces outside the Western Hemisphere. For the next four years, American troops fought in Europe and in Asia, and before World War II was over, more than 400,000 American families were notified that a young person they loved dearly would never be coming home.

And as we know, the end of World War II, in 1945, did not completely put a stop to the fear and dread Americans felt concerning news from other parts of the world, especially from Eastern Europe and the USSR. During the war, the United States and the USSR had been allies in combat, but all along, the U.S. government had been extremely suspicious of Stalin's real motives, and of what he might do once the Axis powers were defeated. Indeed, after the war, the Soviet Union immediately began to drive its influence into Eastern Europe. In 1946, Winston Churchill declared that an "iron curtain" had fallen across the continent of Europe. The metaphor was an extremely effective one; in my childhood, and perhaps in your own, simply listening to adults speak the term *iron curtain* could invoke a cold sense of apprehension that there were children, impenetrably cloaked somewhere, who were suffering and trapped.

Americans heard horror stories about the communist Gulags, where, during Stalin's rule alone, some twenty million people spent time as prisoners in the colonies and camps. The reports were of brutal interrogations, relocations via unheated cattle cars, slave labor, child labor, and mass deaths. The communists deported more than a million Poles to the labor camps of Siberia. They killed hundreds of thousands of people in China. And—most terrifying of all—by 1949, the USSR was able to produce its own atomic weapons. The first nuclear test by the Soviets, "Joe 1," stunned the entire Western world. No one had predicted that nuclear science in the USSR would advance so rapidly. And the grotesque power of that science was vividly fa-

miliar to us, thanks to the publication in glossy American maga-
zines of the "after" pictures of Hiroshima and Nagasaki. As the
editorial pages of our newspapers frantically advocated an immediate preemptive strike against the Soviet Union, many communities across the United States issued dog tags to their young
children, so their bodies could be identified after the war.

Barely recovered from the traumatic stresses of World War II,
and poignantly ignorant of the inescapability of a nuclear aftermath, Americans constructed fallout shelters in their basements
and stocked them with first-aid kits and canned goods. American schoolchildren learned to "duck and cover." American
politicians on the far right referred to liberal reforms, such as
women's suffrage and the child labor laws, as "communist" or
"Red plots." In 1950, Julius and Ethel Rosenberg were arrested
on charges of stealing atomic bomb secrets for the Soviets, vali-
dating our paranoia about secret agents. And our movie screens
and the pages of our science fiction books were populated by
sinister not-quite-human beings who inserted themselves into
our society, bringing with them a clandestine plan to destroy the
American way of life. In short, once again, we were collectively
scared to death. And, as is too often the case, an authoritarian
"leader" was there, ready and willing to direct our fears toward
the advancement of his own personal agenda. During the 1950s
Red Scare in America, the leading fear broker's name was Joseph
McCarthy.

As his career in national politics began, Senator McCarthy, of
Wisconsin, was a popular guest at Washington cocktail parties.
The leading socialites of the day, along with many of his own
aides, described him as charming. But his colleagues in the Senate held a very different opinion. They saw him as temperamen-

tal, impatient. Some even said rageful. They came to dislike him, more or less unanimously, and by the end of his third year in the Senate, he was an isolated figure there.

But all that changed, suddenly and drastically, beginning on February 9, 1950, when, out of the blue, McCarthy delivered a shocking Lincoln Day speech to the Republican Women's Club of Wheeling, West Virginia. Wholly unprepared for this, the club members did not record his address verbatim, but the history books generally agree that, upon taking the dais, Senator McCarthy produced a piece of paper, held it up to be seen by everyone in his sedate audience, and announced, "I have here in my hand a list of 205 people that were known to the Secretary of State as being members of the Communist Party, and who, nevertheless, are still working and shaping the policy of the State Department." There is still an energetic debate as to the exact number cited by McCarthy that day, since later, when he entered the speech in the *Congressional Record*, he said 57 people rather than 205. But no matter. The American press was instantly captivated, and regardless of the particular number of "subversives" supposedly on his mysterious list (which may or may not have existed at all), the McCarthy firestorm had been ignited.

The trauma of World War II was so recent, our terror of communism so great—and the government's need to rally support for the new "cold war" so pressing—that McCarthy's claim concerning communists in the State Department launched him onto a meteoric political path, and nationwide fame. Almost single-handedly, he engendered a frenzy of accusations and investigations that rapidly devolved into the witch hunt that would bear his name into history. In short order, our fear of communism came to be nearly equaled by our terror of Joe McCarthy himself, and the various congressional committees charged with revealing the communist threat he insisted was closeted in the very heart of American society. As we all know, to disagree with McCarthy was to risk being hauled before such a committee, there to be threatened with the label of "subversive" should one refuse to provide the names of friends and colleagues who might conceivably be communists. In many instances, simply being subpoenaed by the House Un-American Activities Committee was sufficient cause to be fired, or to lose a tenured professorship, or to be blacklisted from one's lifelong profession. Almost twelve thousand Americans lost their jobs to McCarthyism, and hundreds of people were imprisoned.

Few mainstream Americans had any exposure to communism as a political philosophy, let alone contact with actual members of the Communist Party. This lack of direct knowledge helped to make plausible the notion that communism was thriving covertly within our own borders. The allegedly grave threat of domestic communism blindsided and completely engulfed us for a time, making us myopic and irrational. The historian Richard Fried has noted extreme instances of our irrationality during McCarthy's reign. For example, the Cincinnati Reds temporarily renamed themselves the Redlegs, so as not to be confused with the other Reds. In Wheeling, West Virginia, where McCarthy had flourished his scandalous list, city officials protested the sale to children of penny-candy wrappers imprinted with miniature maps that sometimes included the Soviet Union. And one Indiana citizen campaigned to remove *The Adventures of Robin Hood* from American library shelves, because the stories it contained explicitly encouraged a subversive leftist strategy—to wit, robbing from the rich and giving to the poor.

Other unreasoned reactions to McCarthy's scare tactics were decidedly less comical. The Robin Hood stories remained on American bookshelves after all, but we removed some thirty thousand other books from overseas libraries run by the U.S. Information Service—books such as Henry David Thoreau's *Civil Disobedience*—after McCarthy's researchers informed us that these were on a list of works written by "communists, pro-communists, former communists and anti anti-communists." And, where our own democratic government was concerned, our fear of communists helped, ironically, to insure that already established domestic and foreign policies would go unchallenged, no matter how inadequate or regressive.

Filmmakers, performers, and artists were particularly targeted by McCarthy. More than three hundred directors, actors, musicians, and writers were denied work in the United States because they were included in an unofficial Hollywood blacklist. Talented and well-known individuals who were blacklisted or otherwise persecuted during the McCarthy era included, among scores of others, Leonard Bernstein, Charlie Chaplin, Aaron Copland, Dashiell Hammett, Lillian Hellman, Langston Hughes, Burgess Meredith, Arthur Miller, Zero Mostel, Clifford Odets, Paul Robeson, Edward G. Robinson, Pete Seeger, Artie Shaw, and Orson Welles.

Arthur Miller, one of the many distinguished writers to be brought before the House Un-American Activities Committee, was sentenced to a fine and a suspended prison term for refusing to apologize to the committee for his interest in Marxist theory when he was a younger man. Afterward, he wrote *The Crucible*, a mesmerizing play about the 1692 Salem witchcraft trials, as a metaphor for the effects of McCarthyism on the American people. The playwright successfully conveyed that falling into a fear-driven madness such as McCarthyism could happen in any era and to any society. In 1996, forty-four years after *The Crucible* first appeared on Broadway, Miller wrote in an article for *The New Yorker* that "the play seems to present the same primeval structure of human sacrifice to the furies of fanaticism and paranoia that goes on repeating itself forever as though embedded in the brain of social man." Miller commented further that the timelessness of his play about a seventeenth-century witch hunt "may simply be a fascination with the outbreak of paranoia that suffuses the play—the blind panic that, in our age, often seems to sit at the dim edges of consciousness."

It is well known that, eventually, McCarthy was not so much defeated as he was vanquished by his own dishonesty and arrogance, and by trying to extend his reach into the military. In 1953, he attempted to discredit Robert Stevens, then Secretary of the Army. President Dwight D. Eisenhower—formerly the Supreme Commander of the victorious Allied Forces in Europe—was incensed, as were others in the Army, who took the occasion to disclose information about McCarthy to journalists known to despise him. The Senate investigations into the U.S. Army were televised, and from their homes, twenty million people witnessed McCarthy's malicious and breathtakingly bombastic performance. Senators on both sides of the aisle were embarrassed before the American people, and on December 2, 1954, by a vote of sixty-seven to twenty-two, the full Senate passed a resolution condemning Joseph McCarthy for abusing his power as a senator and for behavior that was "contrary to senatorial traditions." After that, he remained in the Senate, but was virtually ignored by the White House, his colleagues in Congress, and most of the American media. His career had come full circle, and he was an isolated figure once again, powerless to continue the limbic war he had initiated against his own country. Two and a half years after he was censured, at the age of forty-eight, Joseph McCarthy died of alcohol-induced cirrhosis of the liver.

THE SIX STAGES OF A LIMBIC WAR

These familiar histories—McCarthyism, the World War II internment of Japanese-Americans, and the rise of the Ku Klux Klan after the Civil War—are three American examples of what I have called *limbic wars*. Every limbic war can be divided into six stages. These stages do not have distinct beginnings or ends, but rather merge, almost imperceptibly, each into the next. The first phase always involves a traumatizing event, usually a war or an attack. The five subsequent stages are essentially reactions to the fear instilled in people's minds by the initial tragedy.

Not just in the United States, but in all nations and throughout history, the following are the six overlapping stages of limbic warfare.

1. Group Trauma

A limbic war occurs after some form of national catastrophe. Most typically, this event is a war, or a single attack that is abrupt and brutal enough to generate nationwide fear. The disaster can conceivably be a natural one (such as an earthquake or a volcanic eruption), but natural disasters are less apt to be starting points, since paranoia is less often induced by "acts of God" than by traumatic events brought on by our fellow human beings. Because traumatic memories remain in the brain as incoherent bits of image and sensation that together constitute a neurological trigger—a paranoia switch—the nation that has been traumatized is dangerously reactive to reminders or suggestions of ongoing threat, whether these cues be real, imagined, or contrived.

The Ku Klux Klan drew its first breath just after the American Civil War. The relocation and internment of Japanese-Americans followed the sneak attack on Pearl Harbor. The dark absurdity of McCarthyism was spawned by World War II and our horrified reactions to the subsequent communist atrocities in the USSR and Eastern Europe. The "war on terrorism," along with our current anxiety and paranoia, followed the attacks on the World Trade Center and the Pentagon on September 11, 2001.

In other words, the first stage of a limbic war involves a traumatic event that installs a nonconscious paranoia switch in the minds of a nation's citizens. The second stage requires someone, or several people, to push it.

2. Fear Broker(s)

In Stage 2, one person or a handful of people use the public's fear to pursue a private agenda. These fear brokers are variously motivated. Some, such as the six "founders" of the Ku Klux Klan, discover the extreme vulnerability of the group almost by accident. But, typically, there is a more definite plan, and by far the most common motivators are ambition and a desire for power.

Usually, regardless of their political affiliation or initial place in society, such individuals can be described as *authoritarian*, in the straightforward dictionary meaning of that word: "favoring blind submission to authority," or "favoring a concentration of power in a leader or an elite not constitutionally responsible to the people." Authoritarian fear brokers remind us, frequently and dramatically, of how much danger we are in, whether or not the remaining threat is significant or even real. This technique works well for power-hungry authoritarians. When a paranoia switch is pushed over and over, people are *retraumatized*—they are terrified all over again—and very frightened people tend to be drawn to an authoritarian personality, to someone who insists on making all their decisions for them, who loudly proclaims that he will protect them, and who never admits mistakes. In the upcoming chapter, we will be examining in greater depth this tendency of the frightened to adhere to such "authorities."

This second stage is the all-important one. If leaders willing to use the paranoia switch are not embraced by the people, a limbic war may not occur at all, and the unhappy unfolding of Stages 3 through 6 can be avoided. If they accept the fear brokers, the process continues into its third stage.

3. Scapegoatism

The fear-promoting leader can further heighten the population's anxiety and paranoia by contending that another group or race of people is to be blamed for the crisis. Such a leader may be convinced of the identified group's culpability, or he may be simply opportunistic. However it is motivated, successful scapegoatism slows the group's healing process to a crawl.

At their inception, violent conflicts and wars are caused not so much by the hatreds of the many as by the power and influence of the few. It is not that our hatreds do not exist, but that we could heal them more easily, and drain away much of their poison, without the influence of the few who use hatred's poison as a tool.

This aspect of limbic warfare involves a peculiar twist:

In many cases, the offending out-group designated by a leader is only tangentially, or symbolically—or not at all—related to the disaster that traumatized the nation in the first stage. The KKK targeted African-Americans and other non-whites, and yet these minority groups had not been the invading enemy nor had they caused the wholesale destruction left by the Civil War. Soon after Pearl Harbor, reliable intelligence reports indicated that there was no such thing as a Japanese-American "fifth column." After World War II, there was no vast communist conspiracy in Washington, in our academic community, or in Hollywood. And, of course, we discovered too late that the 9/11 terrorists had not been in league with Iraq, against which nation we unleashed the overwhelming force of our fear and rage.

In this third phase, the leader's focus on retaliating against a scapegoat can confuse the issue to such a degree that the group will be unprepared to protect itself adequately from an actual threat.

4. Cultural Regression

When there is a definite idea of whom to blame, the primitive lust for revenge can crystallize around it. And the idea of a self-righteous vendetta, once it is even whispered of, is a difficult thought for human beings to put away. With all the energy that great fear can generate, the designated out-group is persecuted, or interned, or attacked, and for a time, there is the gratifying sentiment that vengeance is being served.

Typically, encouraging an us-versus-them atmosphere impels a tidal wave of patriotism across the traumatized nation. The new fear-inspired emphasis on national fealty enables the authoritarian leader to divide the population psychologically into two groups: the patriots, who support his authority and his agenda, and the nonpatriots—the traitors, the conspiracy members, the subversives, the cowards—who do not. This division silences alternative ideas and makes true information hard to come by. Paranoia keeps protest to a minimum.

Civil rights are threatened. Humanitarian endeavors atrophy. The arts and literature lose their funding—and their daring. Protected now, intolerance comes out of its hiding places. The limbic war, the emotional manipulation of the people by their own leaders, is in full throttle.

5. Recognition and Backlash

Of the McCarthy era, the playwright and accused subversive Arthur Miller has reflected, "Few of us can easily surrender our belief that society must somehow make sense. The thought that the state has lost its mind and is punishing so many innocent people is intolerable. And so the evidence has to be internally denied."

Fortunately, the evidence is not denied forever. Limbic wars come to an end, and their instigators are eventually deposed. In this stage, protests begin, small and uneasy at the beginning, growing larger and bolder as time goes on. In some cases, a moral red herring is easier for the larger group to rally around than is the main issue. For example, McCarthy's critics began with his drinking, and—as the irony of bigotry would have it—with accusations of homosexuality. (McCarthy, who had persecuted homosexuals with every bit as much fervor as he had devoted to communists, considered a libel suit, but decided against it when told that, once on the witness stand, he would have to answer questions about his sexuality. Instead, he married his secretary, Jeannie Kerr, and the couple adopted an infant girl from the New York Foundling Home.) Regardless of its tangential nature, when a crack has been made in the dam, a general flood of group frustration and anger soon breaks through, and the limbic warrior finds himself swimming for his political life. He will never regain his stranglehold on the country's emotions, and history will tend to judge him harshly.

6. Regret and Forgetting

As the original trauma-engendered fear begins to ease, often years later, we have difficulty recalling why we allowed ourselves to be so easily co-opted into an authoritarian agenda. Many of us are left in a state of dissonance and guilt, and this uncomfortable condition promotes forgetting, a return to the internal denial noted by Arthur Miller. Thus, an experience that might have inoculated us against future problems is effectively lost to us, instead.

This list of six phases introduces many questions. One of the most intriguing of these will be addressed in the next chapter, and pertains to the fear brokers who appear in Stage 2: *Why do nations follow such people?*

What possesses large numbers of people to adhere to someone who is dishonest and, in some cases, absurd? Why can we
not see through such a thin veil? From the perspective of this
new millennium, we look back on Joseph McCarthy, for instance, and we are not sure whether to cry or to laugh. An un-
apologetic bigot, he drank, he ranted, he made accusations that
even a child should not have taken seriously. How could he have
gained such a hold over us? True, we were traumatized by World
War II and fearful of communism and its horrifying reputation,
but were there other factors as well? In such situations—in
all these power plays that hook us by the nature of our own
brains—does something else help to sabotage our rationality?

Yes, something else does, and we confront it head-on in the
next chapter.

SIX THE TERRORIST IN THE CLOSET

As I would not be a slave, so I would not be a
master. This expresses my idea of democracy.

—ABRAHAM LINCOLN

Psychological cruelty craves the dark. Like some inverted car-
nivorous plant, it thrives in the shadows and prefers to blossom
out of sight. Brought into full sunlight, abusiveness shrivels and
dies.

Terrorism is a fine illustration. The seeds of terrorism are
planted and nurtured in the dark. Terrorists do not plan; rather,
they secretly plot. They do not attack; they hide and ambush.
When terrorist cells are exposed, they are rooted out, and when
a terrorist project is brought to light early, it fails. These days, we
are told that the most fearsome terrorists even reside in the dark,
in desolate tunnels and caves.

There are also many nonterrorist examples of the way abuse cleaves to shadowed anonymity, some of them much closer to home. In the United States, for example, Joe McCarthy's destructive agenda succeeded only while McCarthy himself was an enigma to the public—a famous enigma, but an enigma nonetheless. People knew about McCarthy's congressional hearings, and had read about Senator McCarthy in their newspapers for more than four demoralizing years, but not until they viewed the man and his hateful demeanor, in the nationally televised Senate investigations into the U.S. Army, was McCarthy the human being truly exposed. When that happened—when twenty million people saw McCarthy's malicious behavior with their own eyes—his hold over the nation vanished into the thin air from which he had constructed it.

Witnesses, and the clear light of day, are crucially important to our safety from abuse, and anathema to abusers. In *The Wizard of Oz*, the little man in the draped compartment, working the knobs to project the image of a gigantic, frightening wizard, shouts, "Pay no attention to that man behind the curtain!"— because he knows that, as soon as people pull back the drapes, the illusion will be over. Television is a wonderful visual medium for would-be wizards; but also, interestingly, it can be an effective way to throw open the curtains of obfuscation and confront large numbers of people with shocking realities, just as it functioned to unmask McCarthy. This is exactly why the powerful are so careful concerning what our televisions do and do not show us.

The deeply troubling images of the coffins of fallen soldiers—and whether or not these images are allowed to appear on our TV screens—constitute a recent case in point. Understanding the impact of such pictures, the Bush administration banned news coverage and the photography of dead soldiers' homecomings, just before the Iraq war began. In March 2003, as a breathless world waited for the bombs to begin falling on Baghdad, a Pentagon directive to all U.S. military bases stated, "There will be no arrival ceremonies for, or media coverage of, deceased military personnel." The Pentagon was openly aware that images of caskets coming out of transport planes would have an ill effect on public opinion regarding continued warfare, and the administration's ban on taking and disseminating such photographs was carefully enforced, both legally and privately. You may recall the April 2004 news report revealing that, after the *Seattle Times* had published a photograph of flag-draped coffins taken by Kuwait-based cargo worker Tami Silicio, she and her husband, David Landry, were summarily fired by their employer, the Maytag Aircraft Corporation.

The policy has been enforced because it works: "out of sight, out of mind" is apparently a valid assumption where the human cost of war is concerned. Such a ban helps to insure that the full potential of our soldiers' sacrifice never becomes a conscience-galvanizing tableau in our thoughts.

THE "SYNDROME"

Examples abound of how the infliction of suffering survives much longer in secrecy than in public, and the unseen places in which cruelty can remain anonymous are not always exotic caves on the other side of the planet. No, cruelty's hiding places are often very close to us. If you are reading this passage in your home in a residential neighborhood, no matter how upscale, imagine a five-mile radius around yourself (or a five-block radius if you live in a city), and know that sometime very soon, somewhere within your small circle on the map, there will be at least one and perhaps several instances of hidden terrorism. I refer, of course, to domestic abuse, physical or psychological violence done to a person by one of his or her own family members, behind closed doors.

The numbers are astonishing. Nearly one third of American women (31 percent) report being physically or sexually abused by a husband or a boyfriend at some point in their lives. Similarly, around the world, at least one in every three women has been beaten, coerced into sex, or otherwise abused during her lifetime. On average, more than three American women are murdered by their husbands or boyfriends every day, and for women who are pregnant, homicide is the leading cause of death, ahead of car crashes and cancer. The domestic violence statistics for men are less staggering, but men are certainly not exempt. Approximately 15 percent of partner-violence victims are men. To be thoroughly realistic, we must own that the statistics regarding people murdered by international terrorists, though unthinkably tragic, are dwarfed by the numbers of lives shattered and lost through the unseen violence that occurs in the privacy of our own homes.

Though domestic abuse is not the central topic of this book, we can use the small social system of a highly dysfunctional couple to help explain the strange human allegiance to destructive authoritarians in general. The behavior of an abusive spouse, and the other spouse's reactions, can illustrate the answer to the important question posed at the end of the previous chapter: Why do nations of people submit for periods of time to scaremongers such as a drunken, haranguing Joe McCarthy? Why do we not reject incorrigibly self-centered, abusive people out of hand?

Perhaps the most familiar image of the phenomenon now popularly labeled as "abuse" is the woman who is beaten by her partner. There are several other configurations of domestic abuse, the most heartbreaking of which involves children being hurt by trusted adults, but when the term *domestic abuse* is used in social conversation, the allusion is typically to the physical abuse of a wife by her husband. (The reality of a child being intentionally injured at home is too unimaginable, and too guilt-provoking, for most nonabusive people even to talk about, and for this reason, the ongoing epidemic of child abuse is the more securely concealed.) As a therapist for psychological trauma survivors, I have known many such women. I often see them in my practice because, along with a great number of other sad outcomes, one effect of childhood abuse is to make its survivors more vulnerable to accepting relationships with additional abusers in adulthood. As children, we learn our first lessons in love from our parents, and if our parents teach us that love is associated with violence, it is a difficult lesson to unlearn.

In classrooms, during interviews, and sometimes even in social settings, a question I am frequently asked about spousal abuse is one that sounds obvious and simple enough: Why does the victim stay? In other words, once she realizes that the terrible behavior is not going to end, why does she not just get out of there? What could possibly make someone accept such an awful situation? The answer is considerably less obvious and simple, and involves a set of circumstances in which, given a bit of bad luck and lack of knowledge, any one of us might find her- or himself ensnared. This form of psychological entrapment is sometimes referred to as the "battered spouse syndrome," and when I encounter it in my office, the story is often much like my patient Kerry's.

The day thirty-year-old Kerry walked in for her first therapy appointment, precisely on time, her appearance announced that absolutely nothing was wrong. A tasteful black suit was perfectly tailored to her slender body, and her pale hair and pastel makeup were as flawless as any model's. She was soft-spoken and warm, and I liked her immediately. And strangely, when I asked her what problem had brought her to see me, she said, effectively, that there was no problem.

"Nothing's really wrong. Maybe I shouldn't even be here. I just need a good listener for a little while, I guess."

But, as she continued to speak, a picture emerged that was significantly more troubled than her self-presentation proclaimed. During that very first meeting, she shared with me that her father had physically abused her for as long as she could remember, beaten her with a belt and sometimes with his fists, until she was sixteen and had gathered the courage to leave home. In desperation, and with the resourcefulness of someone much older, she had managed to lie about her age and her status in school, in order to get a job as a flight attendant for a small regional airline. She was ashamed of the lie. Also, she told me how soul-splittingly guilty she had felt leaving her mother alone at home, where, Kerry believed, her life was constantly in danger. The mother was regularly assaulted even more viciously than Kerry herself had been, by her own drunken and violent husband.

"That airline job paid pretty well. I kept telling Mom I could pay for things—I could help her get out. But she wouldn't leave, and . . . Well, she's still there."

As Kerry told me this, her gray eyes filled with tears, and soon, her perfect mascara was smeared.

"She used to work at a bank, you know? She was a really classy lady. You just can't imagine the *waste*."

Two years after she left home, Kerry took and passed the GED exam, so that she could truthfully say she had a high school diploma. Feeling she could advance herself in the hospitality industry, she earned an associate's degree at a nearby community college, and eventually became the assistant manager of a three-star hotel in a suburb of Boston.

"I made good money in those days," Kerry said to me. "Or that's the way it seemed to me."

But by the time I met Kerry, she was no longer working. When I asked her why she had given up her job, the answer she gave was ambiguous and troubling.

"I got tired. I just couldn't do it anymore. I mean, all I really wanted was just to give up. I was so exhausted all the time, I even went to the doctor to see if there was something physically wrong. He said he couldn't find anything. So I just resigned. I don't know what's wrong with me. One thing—I think I need a whole lot more sleep than most people."

"Is that why you're here, to find out why you're so tired?"

"No, not exactly. Well, maybe. I don't know." She shrugged and looked down.

She told me that her husband of five years, Vance, worked in various locations as a part-time security guard. I wondered

whether Kerry's success had been threatening to him, influencing her decision to give up her hard-won position, but when I
posed this question (as diplomatically as I could manage), she
said no.

"No, not at all. I mean, I don't really see how that could be.
He was mad as hell when I quit. Vance liked the money I was
bringing in. He said I was lazy for quitting—said we'd go under
financially. But he makes enough to take care of things. He's
kind of a dreamer, but he does okay. And I wasn't going anywhere with that job anyway. He agrees with that. Most of the
people who do really well in management are a whole lot
smarter than me."

By the end of that first session, I had an uneasy feeling about
what Kerry's real problem might be, but I knew she was not
ready to talk about it. I thought about how much courage she
must have needed to walk into a stranger's office, knowing, as
she must have, that she would be able to voice only indirect al-
lusions to her excruciating situation, and tentative requests for
some kind of unspecified help. I hoped her nerve would hold,
and that she would keep the appointment we had made for the
following week. Maybe then she and I could get a little closer to
the truth. As it happened, I could not have appreciated the full
degree of her courage, nor did I anticipate all that would unfold
in a single week's time.

Though she was fifteen minutes late, Kerry did return that
next Monday. But this time, the young woman I found in the
waiting room wore no makeup, and looked as if she had not
even washed her face or brushed her hair in several days. She
had on the same carefully fitted black suit she had worn the pre-

vious Monday, but it had evidently spent the week somewhere crumpled in a heap.

I feared I was about to hear a blood-chilling story from her during the coming hour, and I was right.

She avoided eye contact with me as she walked into my office, and said softly, "Sorry I'm so late."

I said, "I'm glad you're here."

I noticed—it would have been hard not to notice—that now her movements were those of an old woman rather than a healthy thirty-year-old, and she winced and drew in a sharp breath as she sat down in the cushioned armchair across from mine. I tried to reserve judgment, to wait for her to tell me herself why she was in such bad shape, but because I had seen this kind of transformation so many times before, I knew in an instant what had happened. I knew also that this was going to be one of those sessions when I would have to work hard to keep my balance, holding my own sadness and anger in check, in order to be of most help to my traumatized patient. It was maddening; she did not deserve this indignity and fear.

I repeated, "I'm glad you're here. You're hurting. Can you tell me what has happened?"

She made one attempt to deny the obvious, saying, "No, I'm fine." But her situation was unmistakable and unbearable; it seemed to overwhelm her all at once, as if she had used up all her remaining strength just getting herself to my office and into that chair, and as of that moment, the final reserves of her self-control had been spent. Head down, her shoulders heaving with grief, she wept for several minutes, making no sound except occasional soft gasps for air. When the quiet sobbing ended, she folded her hands in her lap and stared at them, and seemed to be scarcely breathing at all. She looked like a female human form out of whom some giant relentless hand had squeezed every glimmer of vitality.

Carefully modulating my voice, I said, "You can tell me about it if you'd like. I'll listen."

After a moment, almost inaudibly, she replied, "But you won't believe me."

I assured her, "Yes, I will."

When I said this, a few more large tears fell from her eyes and splashed onto her folded hands.

Finally, still almost too quietly to be heard, she said, "He hits me. Vance gets really . . ." She censored this second sentence, and after a moment, softly repeated, "He hits me."

When she said nothing more, I prompted her with a question, though I already knew the answer, "Has Vance hit you since we last met?"

She took two long, deep breaths. Finally looking up, she said, "Yes. A couple days after I came here. He found some insurance forms I'd gotten, for therapy, and he blew up. I haven't seen him that mad in weeks." She thought about this for a moment, shook her head, and continued, "Stupid. I was so *stupid*. I could've hidden those papers a whole lot better."

"Vance doesn't want you to be in therapy?"

"Of course not."

"No, of course not," I reflected, almost as if to myself.

When a long-silent victim of domestic abuse finally begins to speak, the truth often comes rushing out in a great flood, frantically propelled by the relief of finding someone who will listen, and possibly even believe. So it was with Kerry. As she told me her story, her voice regained some of its strength, and the words came out faster and faster.

She began, "I didn't know he was like this when I married him, I swear I didn't. I would *never* have married someone like that. Me, of all people. When I first met him, he was charming, I mean *seriously* charming. He made me feel like ten billion dollars. And he was so gentle—no way was this guy ever going to hurt me . . ."

The memory of the nonexistent man she had fallen in love with reglazed her cheeks with fresh tears. Furiously swiping at them with both hands, she pressed on: "Vance is six foot two, shoulders like a brick wall. Not only was I sure he wouldn't hurt me, I kind of fantasized he would protect me—big, strong bodyguard type, you know? Ironic, huh?"

Kerry continued to spill out her truth as rapidly as she could, and the story that soon came together revealed her original confession of "He hits me" to be but a pale euphemism.

When Vance had found the insurance papers, his rage had been instantaneous and white-hot. He had not needed her to tell him what those papers meant. She was getting a little too loose. She was planning to go see some doctor who would want to know secrets, and what Vance did in his own home was private. She was his wife, and his marriage was none of anybody else's business, period. She needed to learn that lesson once and for all, and he knew just how to teach it to her so no one else would see. He would teach her, but there would be no marks on her where anything would show.

Screaming at her about what a stupid, lying whore she was, he pushed her down a flight of stairs to the floor of the living room. After the fall, she could not get up, but she was still conscious, so he kicked her in the body a few times, and then a couple of times in the head—not so hard, though, when it came to the skull, and making sure to aim for the side and the back.

Standing over her, he said, "Don't worry, you stupid little piece of shit—I won't mess up your precious face."

Sometime while he was kicking her head, she passed out.

Kerry told me that afterward, during the night, she kept coming to, only to lose consciousness again. Opening her eyes at one point, she realized she was lying in bed, so she assumed Vance had carried her there; but she was too disoriented to know anything for sure. She woke up completely, with a near blinding pain in her head, at about seven the next morning, according to the clock by the bed. Pushing up into a sitting position was almost impossible, bringing agony to both sides of her body; she was fairly sure some of her ribs were cracked, maybe worse. She was petrified that the beating would start again, but Vance was gone, and on his pillow was a sheet of paper from a yellow legal pad, with a note scrawled in his large, childlike handwriting. She read the note once, and then folded it into a little square.

Later that morning, Kerry managed to get up long enough to hide the little square in the bottom of her purse, where it remained for five days, until her therapy appointment. Now, in my office, she dug into her purse and handed the note to me. I opened all the folds in the yellow paper, and looked up at her to make sure she really wanted me to read Vance's words. Her eyes were pleading.

She said, "Go on. You read it."

And so I read the message Vance had written to his unconscious wife on the morning after he had beaten her:

Dear Kerry,

I am so sorry about last night! It hurt so bad thinking when you see a smart doctor he will tell you I am a bad person!! It made me crazy & I got out of control but I love you so much and if you leave me I think I will die! You know I will never hurt you I mean on purpose and like we talk about all I ever want is to protect you from all the bad guys out there like your dad is. A doctor will not be there and always take care of you and protect you and take care like you know I always will. I will say it again . . . . I am so so so so sorry!!!

Your Husband Who Loves You Forever And Ever,
Vance

P.S. I will get a pizza tonite. No cooking, sweetie!

When I had finished reading, Kerry and I were silent for a moment, and I assumed she was as incredulous and stunned as I was. Finally, she said, "I taught him that word."

"Which word?"

"Protect. I always told him I loved it that he could *protect* me."

"Oh," I said, thinking she was reflecting on one of the many chilling ironies in Vance's message. "It's okay, Kerry. To be protected in certain ways was a normal thing for you to want from your husband. Certainly it was reasonable to want to feel *safe* when you were with him."

She looked up at me, brightening a little, and said, "I'm so glad you think that, Dr. Stout. He really does make me feel safe. I know when he's around, no one can get to me at all, not even my so-called father. He—my father—he hasn't tried to come to the house so far—actually, I can't imagine he ever would—but I know that if he did, he'd never get anywhere near me. Vance would . . . Well, actually, I think Vance would probably kill him."

After Kerry made this statement about Vance eliminating her father, neither she nor I spoke for a few seconds. Apparently, she needed to ponder the frightening and ambivalent image she had just evoked in her own mind. I, for my part, required a moment to reorganize my thoughts, given this abrupt and almost insanely irrational twist in my patient's reaction to being brutally assaulted.

She broke our brief silence, saying, "Obviously I can't protect *myself*. I mean, look at me!" The tears came again as she explained, "I'm so tired and weak. I'm like this idiotic sitting duck! And even if I were in any kind of shape to attract another man—which, as you can see, I sure am not—nobody would ever be as loyal to me as Vance is. And for sure not now—not like this! I'm . . . disgusting!"

As she voiced this opinion, Kerry looked down at her injured body as if it were a form of roadkill that particularly nauseated her. The undeserved self-loathing that flashed across her face inspired a deep sorrow in me, and raised a substantial red flag concerning her compromised chances for long-term survival.

As calmly as I could, I said, "You don't have to live this way, Kerry. I can teach you how to get help. We can talk about how to get you out of this situation. Vance assaulted you, and I'm thinking this was not the first time. It's Vance you need to protect yourself from. Let me help you find a place that's *really* safe."

If our conversation had not been tragic, I could have called it fascinating. Judging from her protestations that she absolutely needed Vance to "protect" her, I concluded that, in some part of herself, Kerry had known before I began to speak, perhaps even before she arrived at my office, that I would say she must remove herself from this dangerous situation with him. But so much fear had accumulated in her life that she would cling to her authoritarian "protector" despite the fact that this "protector" was the very person who had filled her life with fear in the first place, and who would almost certainly continue to do so.

I was sure it had been simple enough for Vance to evoke fear in Kerry. A childhood spent in the house of another violent person, her father, had already taught her that she had reason to be constantly afraid, even—or perhaps especially—in her own home. Her father had installed a paranoia switch in Kerry's psyche. All Vance had to do was push it, by threatening violence himself. He could accomplish this naturally, and without necessarily being aware of any of the psychological dynamics I am describing here. Retraumatized, and convinced that she was too weak, too stupid, and too worthless to defend herself, Kerry would then be ready to deliver unquestioning loyalty to anyone who offered to "protect" her. And the cold logic, the nasty little catch-22, that any person who demands this kind of unconditional allegiance is quite likely to be a perpetrator himself, would be completely outshouted by her widening terror.

Some people never recover from this psychological syndrome, reenacting its vampire-versus-thrall plot over and over, with the same abuser or with a series of abusers, for a lifetime. And some victims do not survive for a full lifetime. (Each year, in the United States alone, two thousand to four thousand women are killed by their partners or ex-partners.) And nearly all of the victims have, at least for a time, viewed their batterer as their best hope and their only champion. A battered human being learns how not to "see" the egregious behavior of her authoritarian partner (typically a characterological type who would never acknowledge his cruelty or his mistakes anyway), and how to construe empty minutiae as evidence that, somewhere deep down, he truly cares. This cognitive distortion sometimes leaves a listener, such as a therapist or a friend, shaking her head in disbelief. As an illustration—Kerry was eager for me to know that, the day after the night that Vance had kicked her to unconsciousness, the pizza he brought home was half and half:

"He ordered a half-plain pizza, for me, even though he would've liked all pepperoni."

It is both a relief and a privilege to report that, in the end, Kerry was able to gather her courage, conquer the irrational belief that she needed an authoritarian keeper, and set herself free. Despite her sad history, despite a neurological paranoia switch installed by childhood trauma, and despite the fact that she had been *retraumatized* on a regular basis in adulthood, she was able to rescue herself. Eventually, she managed to reason her way around the terror and to *think for herself*, rather than continuing to allow her fear-mongering husband to dictate in advance what her thoughts and decisions would be.

Her self-rescue was heroic, but it was not speedy. Before she came to therapy, Kerry had already spent four years with Vance, and he had assaulted her countless times, sometimes giving her a slap in the face and sometimes an all-out beating such as the one she endured when he discovered her therapy plans. Incredibly, during this four-year period, she had taken herself to a hospital for medical attention only three times, the third time at my insistence; in my opinion, that she had survived the marriage at all was a matter of sheer luck. After she came to therapy, Kerry and I met for nearly six more months before she could restore enough faith in her own reactions and judgments to separate from Vance, and then we spent an additional five weeks planning what she began to refer to as her "freedom day." During those five weeks, she gathered her social supports, met with a lawyer, and opened a new checking account in her name only. On "freedom day," to avoid being assaulted again, she waited for Vance to leave for an eight-hour shift, packed a few things quickly, and left without announcement, in his absence. As she had already planned, she drove directly to the home of a good friend, some fifty miles away, where she had been assured she was more than welcome to stay indefinitely if necessary. A week later, she rented an apartment two towns away from the house where she had been paralyzed by fear, moved in, and started her life over again, as a "free woman."

She acquired a restraining order, which she needed to use twice, when Vance, predictably, arrived at her new doorstep. The first time, he shouted obscene insults and pounded on her doors and windows, demanding to be admitted. Kerry called the police. The second time, he stood outside her home, his demeanor contrite, and called to her about how much he loved her and would never hurt her again and only wanted to protect her. Miraculously, Kerry once again called the police. When she told me about this second time, about calling to have Vance removed as he was vowing to be kind to her and to protect her, I knew she was indeed free.

HOW TO RATE A CRYSTAL COFFIN

The psychological recipe that caused Kerry to allow herself to be entrapped and abused for so long is simple, universal, and old. It has three main ingredients. She was (1) predisposed to intense fear (in other words, her brain contained a paranoia switch, in her case because of an abusive father); (2) isolated and "hidden" in a household with her new abuser, away from direct witnesses and the aid of the larger community; and (3) convinced that, in a world so obviously filled with dangers, she needed to be loyal to the person who repeatedly claimed he was the only one who would protect her. It was important to be faithful, to cling to this "protector" no matter what he did, and therefore crucial not to tell anyone—least of all herself—that her "protector" was also a scaremonger, that he was, in fact, the very person now *causing* her to feel so much fear.

Having known so many debilitated survivors, I can attest that controlling injured human beings by means of their reflexive, trauma-instilled vulnerability to fear is cruel in the extreme. This is the case when the perpetrator is the menacing spouse of a childhood abuse survivor, and when the perpetrator is the leader who magnifies the fear of an entire population of vulnerable people in the wake of a national trauma such as 9/11. And one of the most destructive aspects of terrorism resembles one of the most tragic results of childhood abuse. Terrorism, like childhood trauma, sets us up. It makes us intensely susceptible to fear mongers in positions of domestic authority. Following a large-scale terrorist event, brokers of fear in the homeland, much like Kerry's abusive husband, have an essentially easy task: we have already been traumatized, such that little is required to keep us scared. Like Kerry, when we are frightened and paranoid, we are almost irresistibly inclined to be loyal to the ones who say that they, and only they, will protect us. And we try not to let ourselves know that these self-avowed "protectors" are also scaremongers, that they are the very people who are now inflating and maintaining our fears—who are beating us up, so to speak.

After all, our leaders, like our domestic partners, are supposed to be watching our backs, and when we have been terrorized, we will sometimes continue to assume that partners and leaders are so inclined, even in the face of life-threatening evidence that a particular spouse, or a certain leader, has no such caring motivation.

One of the most astounding displays of this human tendency that I have ever witnessed occurred late one summer morning in China's Tiananmen Square. Many Westerners envision Tiananmen with the tanks rolling in on the 1989 student uprising for democracy, and the machine-gun strafing of the defenseless crowds. Tiananmen Square itself is a flat, hundred-acre expanse of stone and concrete; in July, the unshaded sun cooks it as if it were a giant gray pan filled with people. On a normal day, it is brimming, almost as far as the eye can see, with the citizens of Beijing walking busily in all directions, tourists taking photographs and buying souvenirs, tidy lines of schoolchildren, and people flying fierce-faced Chinese kites. The kites resemble mythic beasts hovering above the human activity, and all in all, the scene is strikingly emblematic of China as a whole.

That morning, I observed a barely moving procession of men, women, and children, a waiting line of some sort, so long that it stretched across one entire side of the square and continued out of sight. When I inquired, I was told these were families from

Beijing's countryside, using their new Saturday holiday to wait in the line that led to the tomb of Mao Tse-tung. These thousands of people were willing to stand for two, three, perhaps four hours in the crushing midday sun, for just a moment's glimpse of the reconstituted corpse of Chairman Mao, at rest in a crystal coffin, and to be able to say that their children, too, had seen it. All the summer Saturdays in Tiananmen were like that, I was told.

In life, Mao—"The Great Helmsman"—was a terrifying despot. He controlled all of China from 1943 until his death, in 1976. During his rule, an estimated fourteen million to twenty million Chinese citizens died of starvation. Still more millions of lives were ruined, and tens of thousands of people murdered, as part of his "Cultural Revolution." But he always promised to care for and protect the people he brutalized. The people believed him. Many of them believe him still.

Americans and Europeans are quite able to fall into similar unreasoning patterns relative to leadership, though we are loath to acknowledge this. In 2002, Arnold M. Ludwig, an emeritus professor of psychiatry at the University of Kentucky, published the results of a scholarly analysis of the personalities of 377 leaders from all over the world, including the major contemporary Asian and European leaders and all of the twentieth-century American presidents. For this purpose, he developed a measure called the *Political Greatness Scale* (PGS). The PGS includes factors such as military prowess, success in gaining new territory, ability to establish unprecedented new laws, size of the population ruled, staying power, and legendary status. Ludwig found that a high score on the PGS was correlated with psychological features such as authoritarian dominance, contrariness, "vanity" (meaning, in this case, an inflated sense of self-importance), and a bent to exhibit "wary unease." In other words, statistically—and sadly—the stronger the tendency to dominate, arrogantly and selfishly, and to press the paranoia switch of one's followers, the higher one's final score in political greatness, and this regrettable association apparently holds true all over the world. In human affairs everywhere, there would seem to be a perverse relationship between promoting fear and garnering allegiance.

In Chapter Five, we looked back at some headlines that appeared in the *Los Angeles Times* during the first three months after the Pearl Harbor disaster, just before the fear- and bigotry-motivated internment of 120,000 Japanese-Americans. Now, again with the clearer vision of retrospect, let us review some disturbingly analogous headlines that ran in *The New York Times* during the first fourteen months after the national trauma of September 11, 2001. With a certain compassion for ourselves, we can observe that fear once again became our leading story, along with the usual shades of fear-consolidated allegiance:

U.S. ATTACKED
President Vows to Exact Punishment for "Evil"
[September 12, 2001]

AFTER THE ATTACKS: THE REACTION
For Many, Sorrow Turns to Anger and Talk of Vengeance
[September 14, 2001]

AMERICANS GIVE IN TO RACE PROFILING
[September 23, 2001]

IN PATRIOTIC TIME, DISSENT IS MUTED
[September 28, 2001]

DOCTORS ARE TOLD TO WATCH FOR SYMPTOMS LINKED TO BIOLOGICAL ATTACKS
[October 10, 2001]

ANTHRAX FEARS SEND DEMAND FOR A DRUG FAR BEYOND OUTPUT
[October 16, 2001]

U.S. SEEKS TO STOCK SMALLPOX VACCINE FOR WHOLE NATION
[October 18, 2001]

AFTER A WEEK OF REASSURANCES, [DIRECTOR OF HOMELAND SECURITY] RIDGE'S ANTHRAX MESSAGE IS GRIM
[October 26, 2001]

HOSPITAL WORKER'S ILLNESS SUGGESTS WIDENING THREAT; SECURITY TIGHTENS OVER U.S.
[October 31, 2001]

ASSESSING RISKS, CHEMICAL, BIOLOGICAL, EVEN NUCLEAR
[November 1, 2001]

U.S. HAS COVERED 200 CAMPUSES TO CHECK UP ON MIDEAST STUDENTS
[November 12, 2001]

READMIT INSPECTORS, PRESIDENT TELLS IRAQ; "OR ELSE" IS UNSTATED
[November 27, 2001]

U.S. SAYS THOUSANDS OF LETTERS MAY HAVE HAD ANTHRAX TRACES
[December 4, 2001]

U.S. WILL OFFER ANTHRAX SHOTS FOR THOUSANDS
[December 19, 2001]

IRAQI TELLS OF RENOVATIONS AT SITES FOR CHEMICAL AND NUCLEAR ARMS
[December 20, 2001]

THE ANTHRAX TRAIL
U.S. Inquiry Tried, but Failed, to Link Iraq to Anthrax Attack
[December 22, 2001]

VIDEO CAPTURES SEPT. 11 HORROR IN RAW REPLAY
[January 12, 2002]

BUSH TO REQUEST A MAJOR INCREASE IN BIOTERROR FUNDS
[February 4, 2002]

TERROR SUSPECT SAYS HE WANTS U.S. DESTROYED
[April 23, 2002]

MUSLIMS

How in a Little English Town Jihad Found Young Converts

[April 24, 2002]

CHENEY SAYS PERIL OF A NUCLEAR IRAQ JUSTIFIES ATTACK

[August 27, 2002]

BUSH TO WARN U.N.: ACT ON IRAQ OR U.S. WILL

He Leads Nation in Mourning at Terror Sites

[September 12, 2002]

SCIENCE SLOW TO PONDER THE ILLS THAT LINGER IN ANTHRAX VICTIMS

[September 16, 2002]

SEVERAL NEW METHODS CAN ISOLATE PEOPLE EXPOSED TO CHEMICAL OR BIOLOGICAL AGENTS WHILE THEY ARE TAKEN FOR HELP

[September 30, 2002]

BUSH SEES "URGENT DUTY" TO PRE-EMPT ATTACK BY IRAQ

[October 8, 2002]

CONGRESS AUTHORIZES BUSH TO USE FORCE AGAINST IRAQ, CREATING A BROAD MANDATE

[October 11, 2002]

BEHEADINGS, AMPUTATIONS, REPRISALS: SADDAM HUSSEIN'S PAPER TRAIL

[October 27, 2002]

EXCERPTS FROM NEWS CONFERENCE: IMAGINE "HUSSEIN WITH NUCLEAR WEAPONS"
[November 8, 2002]

IRAQ SAID TO TRY TO BUY ANTIDOTE AGAINST NERVE GAS
[November 12, 2002]

BRITAIN ISSUES FILE ON IRAQ'S "UNIQUE HORROR"
[December 3, 2002]

GUESSING HOW QUICKLY A TERRORIST SMALLPOX VIRUS COULD SPREAD
[December 10, 2002]

FREEDOM DAY

No one knows the complete answer to the problem of human individuals who will frighten and batter members of their own families, even their own children, the very people it should be their great privilege to cherish. Similarly, no matter what any politician or pundit may claim, no one knows how to bring terrorism to a permanent end. Both of these malignant phenomena, domestic violence and political terrorism, are ancient. They have been with humankind since we began to live in groups that were socially and politically organized, respectively. In the fantastically unlikely event that we were able to discover and neutralize—"dead or alive"—every last terrorist now on earth, the time it would take for terrorism to appear again would be only as long as it took for an unfortunate child to be born and grow up with the anger, the ideology, and the sangfroid to plan it once more, and to induct others.

This truth has an intriguing parallel in the one concerning nuclear annihilation that we were taught by Jonathan Schell more than twenty-five years ago, in *The Fate of the Earth*. In 1982, Professor Schell pointed out that, in the improbable case that we completely dismantled every nuclear weapon in every country, the next nuclear threat would require only as long as it took for someone somewhere to design and build a new one.

The potential to destroy ourselves with nuclear weaponry and the ability to commit terrorism—both of these dwell in the human mind, and will be there always. So, in the final analysis, the truth that belies any politician's oath to defeat terrorism is that this is an impossible promise to keep, and an unbounded attempt to do so by physical means would drain even a wealthy nation's resources to the last farthing and the final volunteer. Of course, we can work to lessen the threat of terrorism to ourselves—perhaps substantially if we focus on the task—but we cannot "kill or capture all of the terrorists." Even if we could, the birth of a new future terrorist into deprivation, hopelessness, and rage would occur in the next instant. Deep in its heart, this is not a war between "us" and a separate enemy. This is a collision of values, and a bloody struggle with human nature itself, an ineradicable possibility that can be universally rejected only through cultural and psychological changes in the human race overall.

Until that epoch, you as an individual human being must realize that you already have an illuminating psychological tool for casting some light on both overt and covert terrorism, two of the darkest forms of psychological abuse ever to be perpetrated.

The tool you possess is courage: first, the courage to reevaluate the real physical threat of terrorism to you personally (which, if you are an American, is extremely small, incalculably less than that of dying on a highway, for example), and second, the courage not to be retraumatized and controlled by foreign terrorists—or by political scaremongers right here at home, who are motivated to keep your subliminal fear and your sense of dread at the simmering point. View the information that bombards you with an analytical eye. Do not pledge allegiance to paranoia. Just as it is for a battered and submissive spouse, courageously deciding to get out of a trap built of fear is by far the most knowledgeable, the sanest, and the safest thing you can do.

SEVEN

**FEAR AND THE SOUL
OF A NATION**

Our lives begin to end the day we become silent
about things that matter.

—MARTIN LUTHER KING, JR.

The battered spouse in the previous chapter was abused
by her father in childhood. The American psyche was torn
apart along with the World Trade Center, in 2001. These historical circumstances of trauma provide the first ingredient
for the syndrome of ongoing fear, paranoia, and submission
that we have been discussing. And the vulnerability instilled
by these past traumatic experiences helps to account for the
second component of the syndrome, the rise of authoritarian
"protectors"—the violent spouse, and the various politicians
who fan American fears—and the unshakable devotion these
manipulators enjoy.

But what about the third ingredient, the one that seals the deal of chronic fear and entrapment? What about the *isolation*, the low-visibility conditions, instinctively preferred by traumatizers and retraumatizers, that keep the new abuse invisible and the victims out of rescue's reach? It is not difficult to imagine the isolation and invisibility of spouses living alone together within the walls of a house. But the entire United States? How can hundreds of millions of people, openly going about their lives in the same country, be isolated and hidden from each other?

Mass psychological isolation can and does happen. In fact, it can happen seemingly in the blink of an eye. You and I have recently witnessed an example of this. After 9/11, certain national and racial animosities, usually under cautious wraps in "new-millennium" American culture, sprang above ground and into full poisonous flower almost overnight. Middle Eastern countries, Middle Eastern students and visitors, Americans of Middle Eastern descent, and strangers who so much as *looked* Middle Eastern, suddenly seemed as terrifying as a knife—or a box cutter—to the throat. Within a week, the opinions, beliefs, intentions, and true nature of these communities and individuals became as invisible and inaccessible to the rest of us as landmarks on the dark side of the moon, and our own humanity became equally invisible to them.

And this confused national and racial paranoia is but a circumscribed aspect of the division that befell us. More overarching than racism, the factor that isolated the greatest number of Americans from each other was, of all things, political partisanship. The debilitating intensity of our political prejudices took somewhat longer to develop, months rather than hours, but after they had been pumped to full strength, our ideological passions isolated approximately half of the American people from the other half of us as if we had cracked apart our portion of the North American continent into two warring islands. Historically, Americans have been able to value a certain amount of religious and political tolerance, at least with respect to each other, and the idea of unity is nearly as central to the American mind as that of liberty. But in the months after 9/11, tolerance, and any value placed on unity, deserted us. The dividing line between right and left, conservative and liberal, red and blue became unworkably emotional, humorless, and deeply demoralizing, for both sides. At the moment in our history when it was arguably most crucial for us to work together, instead we fell apart into mutually suspicious "sides," and later discovered that much of the important work had been left undone. Public figures who wished to drum up support for self-centered projects, or to distract us from failures to perform, or from agendas we might otherwise have opposed, could and did succeed by playing off the intense partisan emotions that isolated so many Americans from so many others. And for a long while, leaders who suggested that divisive politics should not be practiced had very few listeners.

You were red or you were blue, and never the twain would meet. And at times, our paranoia about foreign intruders was nearly trumped by our paranoia about our fellow Americans. Not since immediately before the Civil War, when members of Congress came to work armed with pistols, had the country been so emotionally divided along political lines.

The change in our feelings was difficult to describe, but almost palpable. Even for those formerly intrigued by political is-

sues, thinking about them became enervating, depressing. TV
political roundtables became more immoderate and emotional
than ever, devolving into what the University of Pennsylvania
political scientist Diana Mutz refers to as "shout TV," and the
pretense that no one was taking the barbs personally went by
the board. The televised faces snarled, attacked, made us cringe.
The everyday conversations of both Democrats and Republicans
came to be more than a little laced with dread and paranoia. At
a pedestrian stop on a Boston street corner, I overheard a man in
a business suit say to his companions, "Sometimes, I really do
think Bush had a hand in that attack." And between floors on an
elevator in Atlanta, I listened as a flushed young woman, who
was actually trembling, implored the strangers assembled there,
"We've got to do something about Kerry! Do you understand?
If he wins, we're all going to die!"

Why was it so easy to divide the American population after an
event that should have coalesced us like an invasion from Mars?
How did we become so fragmented and antagonistic at a time
when, for example, we could seldom drive a block without encountering *"United We Stand, Divided We Fall"* blazoned on a
car? (In retrospect, the bumper sticker phenomenon would seem
to reflect almost a premonitory instinct that we were about to do
just that: divide and fall.) How did we lose sight of each other so
completely, handing fear mongers their dangerous advantage?

RED AND BLUE GENES

The simple answer is—because the fear mongers wanted it that
way, to enhance their personal or political power. This explana-

tion tends less toward conspiracy theory than it may at first sound. An old and well-known law of power dynamics is that chronically frightened people are easily divided. One of the most unfortunate illustrations of this truism is the case of abused siblings dominated by the same frightening parent. One might imagine that brothers and sisters tormented by a mutual parent would stick together, that they would become closer and more dependent on each other than siblings in nonabusive homes, but in general, the opposite occurs. Clinicians have long observed that the constant fear generated by severe abuse draws and quarters families psychologically, separating even family members who are suffering the same destructive treatment at the hands of the same person. Sudden, acute fear, such as a onetime crisis in a well-functioning family—or a terrorist attack on a nation— can temporarily pull people closer together for support and comfort, just as wartime air raids have been known to make complete strangers fall into one another's arms. But *chronic fear*, a toxic condition that is pervasive and never-ending, erodes and distorts human ties, in a loveless atmosphere of every man, woman, and child for him- or herself.

At the outset, abusers are not necessarily aware of this psychological dynamic, but they do profit from it. Just as there is strength in numbers, there is weakness in being divided. Victims who cannot unite are easier to control than those who can, and a lack of communication among them makes the victimization itself easier for the perpetrator to disavow. In most cases, it is through direct experience that the dominator becomes consciously aware of the advantages of disrupted ties and sympathies, and of the perils of tolerating unity. Following this insight, always keen to promote his power agenda, he may take up measures knowingly designed to alienate and isolate the group's members.

Such a measure does not have to be elaborate or obvious; it can be quick and inconspicuous, like a drop of psychological poison. In a famous scene from the film *The Prince of Tides*, based on Pat Conroy's novel, an unbalanced and emotionally abusive mother whispers to each of her young children separately that she loves him or her best. She ends each disclosure with the admonition "Don't tell the others." In the story, this powerfully divisive tactic is attributed to a lonely, uneducated woman of very few resources. If we extrapolate from this technique, it is unnerving to consider the strategies that might be devised by more sophisticated people—for example, real-life politicians equipped with speechwriters, staffs of political analysts, and television time. It is still more unsettling to realize that, for the purposes of dividing a traumatized nation along political lines, the speeches, the analysts, and the TV messages may be superfluous. In a stressed democracy, when chronic fear is causing ties to break down anyway, influencing people to separate themselves according to the designations of liberal and conservative is not difficult to do. In fact, a high-profile leader in either category would have to work thoughtfully and hard to *avoid* doing so.

We are especially vulnerable in the political domain because, for the human mind, the dimension that runs from extremely liberal on the "left" to extremely conservative on the "right" is a much more fundamental one than we previously knew. Viewed until recently as describing certain attitudes and preferences, and nothing more, *liberal* and *conservative* may now be characterized more accurately as the opposing poles of a *personality characteristic*. A personality characteristic—a "trait"—is an aspect of our permanent psychological makeup that helps to shape our feelings, thoughts, and actions, and that tends to cluster with other, related personality characteristics in complex ways. More encompassing than an attitude or a preference, more lasting than something that we *feel*, a trait is an inextricable piece of who we *are*.

Conceptually, each personality characteristic exists on a continuum, and each person falls somewhere between the two poles that define the ends of that continuum. The poles represent theoretical opposites. So, as classic examples, *introverted* and *extraverted* are visualized as opposite ends of a line along which each of us is located somewhere, according to how inwardly drawn or externally oriented we are. *Impulsive* and *compulsive* occupy the ends of another line, where we each belong on a point according to how freely spontaneous or methodically focused we are. This conceptual structure has been applied to dozens of personality characteristics—ambitious/content, aggressive/mild, risk-tolerant/risk-averse, sensing/intuitive, neurotic/stable, and so forth—that have been studied by psychologists and, more recently, by specialists in heredity.

With the unsurprising exception of a few dimensions, such as neurotic/stable, scientists do not place value judgments on personality characteristics (other than the ancient and wise observation that radical extremes tend to be unhealthy). And left to her own devices, nature would appear to have a gift for balance. A large group of people composed entirely of extraverts all talking at once would be as helpless as a group made up entirely of nonconversational introverts, and a chaotic crowd of acting-out impulsive types as lost as a frozen army of obsessive-compulsives. A well-functioning human group needs individuals from both sides of most personality continua, and in general, the more nearly perfect the balance, the better the functioning.

There is another kind of balance, too, a more mysterious one, between nature and nurture—between *inborn* temperament and *learned* disposition. Are we the way we are for genetic reasons, or owing to environmental factors such as learning? Scientists have found that, for virtually all the personality characteristics they have operationalized and studied, the reliable answer is both. We are the way we are because of genetics *and* through environmental influences. Moreover, the ratio of inborn effects to environmental influences is impressively consistent across most of the psychological characteristics that have been researched. Research by psychologists and heredity spe-cialists, using both adoption studies and identical/fraternal twin protocols, has indicated that, for most personality features, heredity contributes somewhere between 50 and 60 percent of the variance; the environment is thought to account for the rest. To illustrate, according to the available evidence, the degree to which you are introverted or extraverted is a bit more than halfway accounted for by genetics, and about 40 to 50 percent the product of environmental factors.

We do not yet understand all the ways that genetic mechanisms shape the brain—nor how the biology of the brain affects the development of the ineffable mind—and we certainly have not yet fathomed the complex ways in which biological determinants and environmental influences interact to fine-tune particular personality traits. Nonetheless, for most people, the general concept that our personalities are to some degree innate, mysterious as the mechanism remains, is a scientific proposition that comes as no great surprise. After all, parents can corroborate that infants possess distinct temperaments from the day they are born. But, despite our willingness to credit the broad notion of heritability, the specific research that may take some readers aback is a group of studies indicating that *political orientation*—liberal/conservative, left/right—has a genetic component. In other words, new research shows that the tendency for a person to be either liberal or conservative is partly "born in the blood."

In 2005, John Alford of Rice University, Carolyn Funk of Virginia Commonwealth University, and John Hibbing of the University of Nebraska published an article on behavior genetics, using an identical/fraternal twin protocol, in the *American Political Science Review.* These three political scientists analyzed data concerning the political attitudes of a large sample of twins in the United States (specifically, in Virginia and Minnesota), supplemented with findings from a second sample of twins located on the other side of the globe, in Australia. They prefaced their analysis with the comment: "The universal left–right element of belief systems around the world and over the decades is difficult for behavioralists to explain. But if there is a genetic component to political ideologies, if the constraints on belief systems come not just from intellectualization or indoctrination but from something deeper, the concept of ideology takes on greater meaning and the commonality of ideology becomes easier to understand."

Alford, Funk, and Hibbing rated their subjects using twenty-eight items from the *Wilson-Patterson Attitude Inventory* (W-P), which presents a list of stimulus words and asks respondents to choose "agree," "disagree," or "uncertain" for each stimulus. The items used were all related in some way to political ideology: school prayer, pacifism, unions, immigration, women's liberation, the death penalty, censorship, living together, gay rights, abortion, modern art, federal housing, and so forth. (In fact, this subset of the W-P resembles nothing so much as a volatile collection of political "hot buttons.") To derive a "heritability index," the political scientists then applied an accepted mathematical formula to the correspondence of scores for identical twins, who share 100 percent of the variable genetic code, versus the correspondence of scores for fraternal twins, who share, on average, only 50 percent of the variable genetic code.

The logical assumption of behavior genetics is that, for any trait that is at least partly heritable, the tendency for identical twins to share that characteristic should be greater than the tendency for fraternal twins to share it. By this convention, the data of Alford and his colleagues, and the significant heritability index they found in their analysis, indicate that our political attitudes and ideologies are shaped in large part by our genes. More research is needed, but the findings of this study already suggest that the heritability figures for political orientation fall into the same range as those for the other, more traditional psychological characteristics that have been investigated.

This discovery about our inborn "politics" stands to alter much of what we thought we knew about the nature of ideological thought and behavior. Alford and his colleagues believe their data point to two "broad but distinct political phenotypes." They write that one of these would seem to be characterized by a relatively strong suspicion of out-groups, a yearning for in-group unity and strong leadership, a desire for clear and unbending moral and behavioral codes, a preference for swift and severe punishments for violations of these codes, a fondness for systematization, a willingness to tolerate inequality among groups, and a fundamentally pessimistic view of human nature. The other phenotype would seem to be characterized by relatively tolerant attitudes toward out-groups, a desire to take a more context-dependent rather than completely rule-based approach to proper behavior, a fundamentally optimistic view of human nature, a distaste for preset punishments, a preference for a group to-getherness that overlooks differences, suspicion of hierarchy/ certainty/strong leadership, an aversion to inequality, and greater general empathic tendencies.

The political scientists who conducted the study point out that common political usage would call the first category "conservative" and the second "liberal." But their own goal is to find alternative expressions "that are less connected to political ideologies and that indicate that these two phenotypes run to the very orientation of people to society, leadership, knowledge, group life, and the human condition." With this goal in mind, they propose the term *absolutist* for the first category, and the term *contextualist* for the second.

Adopting the conceptual structure offered by psychology, we can use these findings and terms to suggest a new personality characteristic, one that can be visualized as a continuum with an anchor of *absolutist* on the right and *contextualist* on the left. As with most traits, except for its extremes, this continuum would bear no value judgments, just objective links with other personality characteristics and with orientations toward other human concerns. According to Alford and his colleagues, this new absolutist/contextualist dimension may well be related to what the authors call the "basic cleavages" in such concerns as religion (fundamentalist/secular humanist), art (form-based realistic/ free-form modernistic), medicine (conventional/wholistic), and ethics (invariant applications/situational reasoning). As a psychologist, I might add to this list an area of study from developmental psychology, that of moral development (societal rules/personal responsibility).

Alford and his colleagues write: "In our view, all of these vexing perennial dichotomies are related cultural expressions of a deep-seated genetic divide in human behavioral predispositions and capabilities." In light of their genetic data, they believe the "chasm" that isolated half of all Americans from the other half in the early twenty-first century was not a division between supporters and opponents of privatized Social Security, or those of gun control, or those of same-sex marriage, or those of any other policy issue. Rather, the rift was a more fundamental one—between absolutists and contextualists. They point out that the differences tending to "hit people in the gut" are innate ones—differences not in what they believe, but in *who they are*—and remind us of the frustrations that most of us, on both sides of the continuum, have experienced at one time or another: ". . . to contextualists, absolutists appear simplistic and selfish; to absolutists, contextualists appear naive and indecisive."

I liken this situation to a bizarre imaginary fight to the finish between introverts and extraverts for control of a country. Using this metaphor, we see that such a struggle involves at least three major fallacies. First of all, no one is going to convert to the other side, because no one can change herself or himself from one partially innate personality type to another, even if she or he wishes to do so. Second, the lifelong inner reality of introverts is so different from the lifelong inner reality of extraverts, and both inner experiences are so fundamental, that any value-laden debate on the subject of introversion/extraversion will quickly become raw and emotional, rather than rational or productive, from either vantage point. (I should note that most people would never join such a debate to begin with, not even in their imaginations, because most of us understand that introversion and extraversion are aspects of a person's psychological makeup, not positions that can be judged by their logic or expediency.) And third, and perhaps most significant, *there is no point* in raising either introversion or extraversion to a dominant position. One is not better than the other, or inherently a threat. The two types are simply different. Moreover, nature's balance between introverts and extraverts probably creates a more functional group. In parallel fashion, to quote Alford, Funk, and Hibbing, "As loath as contextualists and absolutists are to admit it, the presence of the other orientation may make a society stronger."

Chronic fear divides and isolates people, in families and in nations. In the United States, the great rumbling fault line between Republicans and Democrats is an especially sensitive one for fear politicians to bear down on. Whether the method is planned in advance by political strategists, or is merely the eventual discovery of an unethical leader—who, like an abusive parent, has learned the power advantages of keeping his or her victims separated—to stress differences that feel like part of *who we are* is a cheap and easy way to make us lose our national balance.

Declining popularity? Distract both foes and friends with a speech on a divisive subject such as gun control. Are the people beginning to unite against you over a central issue? Deliver a diatribe about same-sex marriage—not part of the same central issue, but a topic known to jab painfully at the fundamental differences between conservatives and liberals. Say to your constituency, in effect, *Let's you and them fight.*

Such tactics of distraction and division help to conceal a power play that I call *cowbird politics*, after the little North American "brood parasite" that makes no home for its offspring, preferring instead to lay its eggs in the nests of other birds, who will be confused but far more responsible than the cowbird. A cowbird politician, who is interested only in acquiring and maintaining individual power, has few genuine convictions, either liberal or conservative, but may be ensconced in a traditional political party (as Joe McCarthy was, for example). The purloined "nest" serves as a power base and also as camouflage; we tend to honor party labels and not to look behind them, making pure self-interest difficult to see. But cowbird politicians, regardless of which political banner they wave, are definitely not team players. They are often the most divisive leaders of all, because, behind the camouflage, their agendas are not prescribed or limited by any philosophy or system of values. They can and do use the hammer of fear politics for their own purposes, ignoring protest from both halves of the political continuum.

Typically, the unspoken subjective experience of a cowbird politician is that of traveling high above such categories, in a flight path that will tolerate no redirection. For a period of time, this lofty and single-minded trajectory can appear heroic to the populace, until, upon closer inspection, the high-flying cowbird is revealed to be not so much free of political constraints as he is emotionally untethered from important group concerns.

DIVIDED WE FALL

Set up by traumatic experience, and dominated by a new abuser who controls her with fear, isolates her, and demands her silence, a battered spouse soon falls into a downward spiral involving all aspects of her life. Her health will suffer, and not just because of the beatings. Chronic fear itself will take its toll on her immune system, her cardiovascular system, and her mental acuity. At first, she will feel demoralized and trapped in her passivity, then severely depressed and paralyzed. To herself, and also to others, she will begin to seem a mere ghost of her former self. If, earlier in her life, she was intelligent, articulate, interesting, creative, these positive characteristics will be dim memories at best. Eventually, and most ruinously, the bottom-line responsibilities and values that used to guide her life will fade, as well. If she has children, getting them out of harm's way, or even caring for them on a day-to-day basis, may require more planning and strength than she can muster. When she sees this final deficiency in herself, shame will overwhelm all remaining initiative.

An entire nation that has been traumatized and that is now directed by fear politics, one in which population groups are deeply divided and isolated, will follow a course that is disturbingly parallel to that of the battered spouse. This can be said of Americans, we who are traumatized by terrorism, suffering the further destructive influences of far too many fear politicians, and more emotionally divided along political lines than we have been since the Civil War. For many of us, the internal image of our country as it was before 9/11 feels like a fading memory. Our passions—our inclination to protest and our energy to express ourselves intellectually and creatively—have lost some of their historical intensity. Worst of all, our world-renowned insistence on liberty and human rights has been temporarily muted by our fears, and by those who would encourage our fears. Few conditions—even the extraordinary passivity of a battered spouse—seem as inexplicable as this sudden meekness in millions of famously strong-willed people.

Soon after September 11, 2001, our liberties were restricted in many ways, and in a disaster-driven panic to be protected, we offered little protest. Some of the more controversial limits on our privacy and civil rights involved an expansion of the government's license to monitor and conduct undercover infiltrations of political and religious groups, and the granting to the government of an unprecedented authority to eavesdrop on privileged attorney-client communications. Significant limitations were placed on the scope of the Freedom of Information Act. We ceded to the government a greater authority to conduct covert reviews of online communications, including e-mail, and to carry out secret reviews of banking and other financial records; we granted it increased authority to perform clandestine physical searches and expanded its powers to wiretap and to engage in electronic eavesdropping. In addition, new legislation supported the indefinite detention of more than a thousand noncitizens, individuals who were in the United States lawfully and who had not been charged with any crime. These detainees were given no access to judicial review. The government maintained a blanket secrecy regarding their identity, and refused to allow many of them to communicate with an attorney.

The USA PATRIOT Act was presented to Congress only six weeks after the calamities of 9/11, with then Attorney General John Ashcroft ominously characterizing as "soft on terrorism"

anyone who questioned its constitutionality. In grief, and terrified like everyone else, the members of Congress passed the
legislation immediately, and beginning with that congressional
decision, fear and the desire for renewed security became the
motivating forces behind most changes in American law. However, a year later, by the time Ashcroft announced he was about
to institute a new Terrorism Information and Prevention System
("Operation TIPS") that would call on U.S. citizens to monitor
and report on other U.S. citizens, many Americans were already
growing concerned about the precipitous erosion of their civil
liberties. Congress raised objections, and Ashcroft withdrew the
proposal.

Though we do not enjoy recalling the episodes in our history
that veer away from our shared principles, we know that the aftermath of 9/11 is hardly the only time the American government has limited our freedoms, and then suppressed dissent, in
the name of national security. In his book *Perilous Times: Free
Speech in Wartime*, Geoffrey R. Stone, a former dean of the University of Chicago Law School, discusses the American struggle
to balance liberty and security, from the Sedition Act of 1798 to
the "War on Terrorism." The word *fear* appears on more than a
quarter of this lengthy book's pages. Stone recalls the years of
the Vietnam War, when the FBI conducted an extensive program to "expose, disrupt and otherwise neutralize" dissidents,
and the federal government attempted to prevent *The New York
Times* and *The Washington Post* from publishing the Pentagon Papers. Later on, the FBI's attempt to "neutralize" (frighten, disrupt, or discredit) protesters was denounced by Congress and
the Department of Justice.

Stone speaks of McCarthyism and the House Un-American

Activities Committee during the Cold War, and of the internment of Japanese-Americans during World War II, during
which era the federal government sought to silence criticism by
prosecuting and sometimes deporting those who openly questioned the war. And he reminds us that the American government took some two thousand people to court for their
opposition to World War I, including the 1912 Socialist Party
candidate for the presidency, Eugene Debs, who was sentenced
to ten years in prison for his public denouncement of the war
and the draft. In long hindsight, we can see that President
Woodrow Wilson needed to foster a climate of fear and outrage
so that Americans would remain at war, despite the fact that
they had been neither attacked nor threatened with attack.

The examples from our history continue into a long and eye-
opening list of fear-driven instances when the First Amendment
has been either distorted or completely ignored. But the American commitment to free speech is crucial not only because it
protects our personal rights, but also because it supports the
continued functioning of democracy itself, *especially* in times of
war. Protected free speech helps a nation make wise and temper-
ate decisions even under stress, and enables open and informed
discussions about how adequately our leaders are performing
and concerning when a war should end. Stone points out that
democracies often fare better in lengthy wars than do dictator-
ships exactly because all members of a democracy have the right
to voice their ideas. And he tempers this optimistic commentary
with a 1951 warning from Justice Robert H. Jackson: "It is easy,
by giving way to the passion, intolerance and suspicions of
wartime, to reduce our liberties to a shadow, often in answer to
exaggerated claims of security."

In sum—during a number of fear-provoking crises in American history, we have been promised protection if we would relinquish some of our government's balance of power and a few of our liberties. Often, we have gone along with this questionable deal, and always, in the end, we have regretted the arrangement.

In the years that followed the destruction of the World Trade Center, changes in our nation's attitudes toward privacy and free speech were joined by regrettable shifts in other treasured aspects of our society. Even religion, to which so many people had turned for guidance and comfort in 2001, began to feel the denaturing influence of protracted fear. The defining grace and loving-kindness of religious and spiritual thought was often outshouted by television preachers and extreme fundamentalists. These sometimes highly funded religious leaders took the occasion of 9/11 to terrify American believers, and indeed, anyone anywhere who would listen, by aligning terrorism in the United States, along with violence in the Middle East, with the prophecies made in the biblical book of Revelation and with personal prophecies of their own. They encouraged gruesome fantasies of the "End Time," and preached that their followers—and only they—would survive the imminent apocalypse. With renewed zeal, they taught hatred for members of religions other than their own, and, most of all, for the followers of Islam.

After Muslims on the hate list were environmentalists, humanists, homosexuals, scientists, and a formidable inventory of other groups. To the most extreme fundamentalists, environmentalists were especially objectionable, since their desire to protect the earth reflected a lack of faith in the imminent cosmic cataclysm, in which God would raise the righteous to heaven.

End-Time preachers and politicians advised their followers that reports of environmental decline should be regarded as good news, simply part of the prophecy, and that while the righteous were still on earth, God would provide sufficient clean water and fossil fuels for them, much as He had miraculously provided an abundance of loaves and fishes for the multitudes.

A few famous religious leaders claimed to be in special communication with God, and eventually, some of our secular leaders began to imply the same of themselves. A politician could suggest, by his demeanor, or by certain religious analogies, or in some instances quite directly, that he was sent by God to save good people from terrorism, and what might have seemed megalomaniacal or crazy to us in the past, when we believed we were safe, somehow felt almost comforting in a time of fear. There are no atheists in foxholes, or very few, and when the world becomes terrifying, evidently even the sane may tolerate a subtle messianic cadence in the speech of a leader.

Many Christians protested, declaring that theological discourse and the moral values of Christianity had been co-opted. In 2005, Ed Bacon, the rector of the All Saints Episcopal Church, in Pasadena, California, asserted in an interview that self-interested TV personalities, along with a number of the nation's politicians, had "hijacked the Bible and Jesus and got us focused from a fear-based perspective on one or two wedge issues." Jim Wallis, evangelical Christian and author of *God's Politics: Why the Right Gets It Wrong and the Left Doesn't Get It*, expressed the same concern in his book: "Many of us feel that our faith has been stolen, and it's time to take it back . . . How did the faith of Jesus come to be known as pro-rich, pro-war, and only pro-American? What has happened here?"

In the same thin atmosphere of constantly encouraged fear, the arts began to suffocate, as well. The United States is blessed with an abundance of preeminent theater groups, musicians, dance troupes, folk artists, visual artists, and art museums. But sadly, and unsurprisingly, the week of September 11, 2001, saw the most precipitous drop in theater attendance in our history, and that week marked only the beginning of demoralizing financial difficulties for the American arts. The three major financial pillars of the arts—government funding, charitable donations, and earned income—all began to fall away. In 2003, arts agencies in forty-three out of fifty-six state and territorial agencies suffered serious decreases in their general fund appropriations. In 2004, thirty-four agencies reported cuts, nine of them by more than a third. And as I write, financial support for the arts—considered a frivolous expenditure by a still frightened nation—continues to decline.

In meaningful contrast, during this same time period, gun sales increased by as much as 50 percent in some states, and according to FBI reports, background checks for handguns also rose dramatically. Especially in 2005, after Americans viewed the retraumatizing televised images of New Orleans in the wake of Hurricane Katrina—the ubiquitous looting and the human chaos that our infrastructure had not been prepared to handle—gun ownership enjoyed hugely increased popularity.

Guns did well, but academic freedom suffered along with the arts, theology, and civil rights. Books became the enemy in a way they had not been since the 1950s, when McCarthy insisted that "subversive" volumes, such as Thoreau's *Civil Disobedience*, be removed from U.S. Information Service libraries. As an illustration of this aspect of our societal fear reaction—in 2002, citing that the University of North Carolina's fall reading list for freshmen had included a book about the Koran, the North Carolina legislature attempted to cut the university's budget. After we were assured that we were waging a "war on terrorism," there were certain ideas that academics were simply not supposed to express. For example, the American Council of Trustees and Alumni (ACTA) took to task a professor of religious studies at Pomona College for stating that "we have to learn to use courage for peace rather than war."

Freedom of scientific inquiry was threatened, as well. The U.S. Department of Education moved to eliminate from its website all links to scientific researchers whose policies did not agree with those of the administration, and a new website was established to monitor educational institutions and faculty who were critical of U.S. policy or action in the Middle East. The Office of Homeland Security revealed its wish to limit scientific publishing, especially the publishing of methods and data sets that could lead to replicating results. (Anyone who has learned the basics of the scientific method will protest instantly that such a limitation would bring scientific progress to a halt, as one of the key functions of publishing is to provide methods and data sets to other scientists for the specific purpose of attempting to replicate results.)

In retrospect, we can see that our abrupt nationwide switch to paranoid anxiety caused us to compromise values that live at the very heart of the American dream: unity, liberty, tolerance, freedom of thought and of speech. Did this psychological and spiritual decline in our society "work" for us? In exchange for our sacrifices, were we provided with greater security? No, we eventually discovered that this was not the case—indeed, not even close. Federal reports in 2006 disclosed that, though the National Security Agency had monitored the phone calls of two hundred million Americans in what it hoped would be "the largest database ever assembled in the world," only six of seventy-five U.S. metropolitan areas (8 percent) had won the highest grades for their emergency agencies' ability to communicate during a disaster, five long years after the September 11 terrorist attacks. The Department of Homeland Security offered the breathtakingly understated explanation that "formalized governance (leadership and planning) across regions has lagged."

If the United States were a psychological trauma patient, at this point I would tell her that, to complete her recovery from the monstrous assault on her by outside terrorists, she must learn how to identify and deal with domestic fear brokers, with the current and future perpetrators who would retraumatize her and keep her in a state of division and subliminal fear—those who would use her legendary strengths not for her true goals, but for their own ambitions. And so, in the next chapter, I will describe—in clear and abundant detail—what such perpetrators are like, how they speak and behave, so that the next time you see one on television, or anywhere else, you can say to yourself, *That person wants to control me with fear.*

Equipping yourself with the ability to recognize fear mongers is a direct and highly effective approach you can take to safeguarding the eternally paired values of freedom and democracy, and toward making yourself feel at home again in your own country. I should forewarn you that learning this lesson requires more moral courage than most people imagine.

EIGHT WHY WE CANNOT SEE THE DEVIL

Sometimes

The Devil is a gentleman.

—PERCY BYSSHE SHELLEY

esperate, nearing the end of her third abusive relationship, a thirty-year-old childhood trauma survivor asks, "Why do I always get hooked up with these men? Does something about me make them want to hurt me? Or does something make me keep falling for people like this? Once is maybe bad luck or something, but this is my third time! What's wrong with me?"

A talented but depressed high-tech entrepreneur says, "This is the second bookkeeper who's burned me—the second in a row! Why don't I learn? By now, you'd think I could see it coming a mile away, but both times were real shockers for me. As a matter of fact—well, this is a laugh—I thought the second guy was even more worried about security than me. He actually told me I wasn't being careful enough when it came to personnel."

An anxious eighty-year-old woman, recently widowed, reports that her friend's grandson, a "very smart young man," has been visiting her home and has become concerned that she does not know enough about finances to handle her affairs. "He said I could lose all my money if I did the wrong things. I started to get awfully scared about that. My little nest egg is all I've got. He said if I'd pay him two thousand dollars, he'd take care of all the papers for me. And I've got to go through some things and find the key to my safe deposit box at the bank, so he can check on that, too."

In mid-September 2001, millions of shell-shocked Americans watched news reports about sidewalk swindlers descending on Ground Zero in New York. Very troubled, one of my trauma patients said to me, "On TV, they don't look like ghouls. They look like ordinary people. To me, that's the creepiest part."

The people who profit from our fears, and who exacerbate our paranoia and dread, do not wear signs that say FEAR BROKER or RETRAUMATIZER. Often, these opportunists seem normal, so normal, in fact, that their potential for doing us harm can be invisible. Their best chances to manipulate and rob us derive from the aftereffects of abuse, recent trauma, and loss. Seldom do we see the new calamity coming. The perpetrator offers himself as a protector or a helper, taking advantage of our heightened need for protection and assistance. It is only in retrospect, and then only sometimes, that we recognize what he was, and how he went about using us in a time of need.

Once again, Joseph McCarthy can serve as an illustration. He drew his power from our collective paranoia during the Cold War that followed World War II, proclaiming—if not credibly, then at least loudly—that he would rid us of the clandestine traitors in our midst. And, in 1954, his tyrannical hold over the nation fizzled rapidly, with a whimper and not with a bang, when millions of television viewers saw the true McCarthy with their own two eyes and realized that they had been deceived. Still, many years would pass before we began to comprehend that it was almost exclusively our fears that allowed him to do what he did. We were vulnerable, and McCarthy was simply there.

From our new understanding, many "what if" questions arise: What if we *could* see them coming? What if we could recognize the Joseph McCarthys of the world—and the lesser fear brokers, con artists, and abusers—before they had the chance to mount podiums constructed of our fears? What if people could have diagnosed and dismissed McCarthy as shameless and pathetic as soon as he played his first sensationalistic hand, on that February day in 1950 when he melodramatically pulled out a list of people he claimed were "card-carrying communists" in the State Department? Or, better, what if people could have understood his true nature four years before that, when he ran for a Senate seat using campaign posters of himself in full World War II fighting gear, along with multiple ammunition belts and a claim to have flown thirty-two missions—when, in fact, he had held a desk job during most of the war? What if Joseph Mc-Carthy's name were not in our history books at all? It is impossible to estimate how many people's lives would have been better, would have contained less tragedy. Even now, how many of their children and grandchildren would have more luminous life stories to tell? The damage done by McCarthyism, to individuals and to our society as a whole, radiates beyond imagination, and so would the erasure of it from history.

Of course, when all of history and all nations are considered, McCarthy was just one tyrant among a great many such, and not even close to the worst. What if we could identify some of the world's scaremongers and disempower them before they left indelible marks on us, and on our children's children? In more ways than we could count, would we not be elevating the human future, and our self-regard as a species? We could inaugurate a miraculously hopeful circle, in which fewer paranoia switches would be pushed, creating fewer human conflicts—and so, in time, fewer hardwired fear reactions in the first place. How much heartache could be avoided in this way? How many wars? How much less willing would we be, in all nations, to allow the priceless flesh and blood and futures of our daughters and sons to disappear into the black hole of the fear brokers' unending battles?

We have no way of knowing whether humanity will ever reach this triumphant point in its development. An era of healing from past traumas would have to occur first, and it is exactly this healing process into which scaremongers perennially insert tragic delays. Perhaps we will enter a more hopeful pattern during this new century, or this new millennium. And, regardless of whether or not we use the information to safeguard ourselves from them, it is quite possible—here and now—to *identify* many contemporary fear politicians and would-be opportunists, the potential McCarthys. To demonstrate that we already have this "discovery" capability, I will show you a list of ten recognizable earmarks of scaremongers in public life. The list is straightfor-

ward, and after you have read it carefully, most of the characteristics described here will be easy to detect in the real world.

In *The Sociopath Next Door*, I coined the first psychological
definition of conscience, which is an intervening sense of obligation based in our capacity to form emotional attachments. I
used this definition in my discussion of *sociopathy*, which is the
deeply pathological condition of possessing no conscience what-
soever. But I would like to point out that the fear politicians
whose characteristics I list here are not necessarily sociopathic.
In other words, not all fear politicians are devoid of conscience.
When a leader behaves so as to inflame the post-traumatic fears
of his or her followers, conscienceless self-interest may well be
the reason, but other explanations must be considered, also. For
example, an extreme ideologue—someone whose interpersonal
attachments, though they exist, are less compelling for him than
his obsession with a system of ideals—may deem it necessary to
use the people's fear in the service of the cause he considers all-
important. A variation on this pattern is the neurotic leader
whose early background exerts psychological pressure on him to
achieve a particular goal. This sort of leader, too, may believe it
acceptable to fire up and use the people's fear to serve the cause
that drives him. Another leader may have a deep-seated desire
for revenge, a desire that he wishes to instill in the people and
then to prosecute as a popular cause. Yet another type of leader
may suffer not from run-of-the-mill neurosis, but from paranoid
psychosis, in which case he may preach fear with the hypnotic
oratory of madness and delusion. This last category is especially
dangerous, since intelligent paranoids, in both private and public
life, are often astute enough to conceal their craziest suspicions
from other people and to make their more moderate delusions

sound almost reasonable. It has been argued that many of history's most genocidal tyrants, the worst of the worst, have belonged to this group.

Any of these conditions, alone or combined with the sociopath's lack of conscience, may lie behind the behavior of a dedicated fear politician (or, interestingly, behind the activities of a terrorist). But a ruthless lust for power, vengefulness, ideological obsession, neurosis, and even psychosis can be difficult to detect, especially from a distance. For this reason, a scaremonger's underlying motivation, though intriguing, cannot be our first concern. Much more practical would be some behavioral attributes, which are easier to discern from far away, from television broadcasts and newspapers. And so, here is the list.

TEN BEHAVIORAL CHARACTERISTICS OF FEAR BROKERS

1. Fear brokers speak to us of fear, dangerous people, and frightening situations.

This first characteristic might seem too obvious to mention, except that we often overlook it in our day-to-day lives. When we are awake and alert, it is our natural inclination to push our various anxieties away from conscious thought, so that we can carry on with our normal activities. Add to this our vanity, since almost no one would wish to view him- or herself as easily frightened, and certainly not by events so trivial as political speeches and newspaper articles.

Then, too, the "broker" is rarely foolish enough to speak exclusively of fear, because an undiluted harangue about danger rapidly becomes overwhelming and alienating. When addressing the public, he will raise subjects other than fear. These are often flattering topics, intended to showcase the people's superior bravery and nobility (that is to say, superior to those of other groups of people). He may even use humor. But somewhere within virtually every address, there will be several references to danger, and to just how frightened people must not forget to be.

Immediately after listening to a fear broker speak, you may feel slightly unsettled, or as if your equilibrium or mood is not quite the same as it was prior to his remarks; but in the moment, you probably will not be able to pinpoint exactly why, or even what the feeling should be called. This subtle inner shift will occur regardless of where you stand on the political continuum. (Fear is fear, labeled or unlabeled, and whether you admire the messenger or not.)

2. Fear brokers are not limited by facts; they use alarming "unfacts."
True scaremongers do not wait for outsiders to cause additional psychological vulnerability. Rather, scaremongers assume for themselves the job of retraumatizing us, and in doing this job, they are not hindered by the known facts.

Where terrorism is concerned, out-and-out lying may not be required. It is easy enough to fan public fears by giving alarming renditions of terrorist events that *might happen* in the future, and by speaking in imaginative detail about terrorist events that *would have happened* had they not been thwarted. When such "unfacts" are delivered dramatically, there is seldom any prosocial motive involved, only the intent to capture an audience and amplify fear.

The delivery of an "unfact" about terrorism offers an advantage to the fear broker that repeating a fact about terrorism would not, which is that one can boundlessly exaggerate an "unfact," and it will still have the ring of truth. Attacks that *might happen* or that *would have happened* can be as cataclysmic as the speaker wishes them to be, and most can be attributed to any cryptic agent the speaker deems useful to his agenda—and all without the risk of being caught in a technical lie.

When someone often uses frightening "unfacts," it is reasonable to wonder whether he or she is brokering fear.

3. Fear brokers tend to accuse those who disagree with them of being unpatriotic and/or naive.

When you are wondering about scaremongering, listen for the use of these particular insults. They work extremely well, in part because they are especially sticky in a time of national crisis, and in part because they communicate self-defining ideas to the people who are listening. The tacit messages to the fear broker's audience are as follows:

"You [unlike him/her/them] love your country," and
"You [unlike him/her/them] understand that it is wise to be suspicious and fearful."

4. Fear brokers look good.

Most of us have grown up with storybook and TV images of bad guys who look like bad guys, shifty-eyed and unappealing. But, perhaps ironically, a scaremonger cannot afford to have shifty eyes or scary teeth, or any other seriously repellent feature, unless his audience never sees him (an unlikely degree of anonymity in the twenty-first century). No, just like the broker of some commodity much finer than fear—art, boats, invest-

ments, houses—the broker of fear must be attractive. This is because, other factors being equal, an attractive person is perceived
as smarter, more honest, and more trustworthy than an unattractive person.

Of course, not everyone is blessed with physical beauty, and
in any case, beauty is in the eyes of its beholders. Because we
love the familiar, a fear broker who is not a natural head-turner
can make himself attractive by looking *as much like the people in
his constituency as possible.* In the United States, to look like the
people in one's constituency means to appear and act like the
girl or the boy next door, the prototype of the wholesome,
well-scrubbed American, the president of everyone's high school
student council, all grown up.

It is important to appear educated, but not too worldly or
glib. Common sense is important, and a certain amount of intelligence, but undisguised genius will cause one to be perceived as
arrogant and not "of the people." A kind of down-home charm
is helpful, and as it happens, many of the behaviors considered
to be charming can be learned: flattering people, making eye
contact, smiling, nodding one's head in apparent interest, echo-
ing the concerns of others. If one is from a region where the
people speak with a "heartland accent," that accent can be nurtured.

If all this sounds to you like a recipe from a cynic, know that
you are evaluating the description accurately. This formula for
self-presentation serves an ambition to be trusted for no good
reason, and an overarching aim to manipulate people with their
own fears, which are indeed cynical approaches to one's fellow
human beings. That many followers will suspend their disbelief
when presented with an overacted performance is rooted in an

ancient mental reflex to view the world in terms of "us" (the familiar folk) versus "them" (all those who are different). Accepting the leader's cynical mimicry allows people to feel included as near equals with the powerful—and to feel safe from "them."

5. Fear brokers behave like archetypal parents.

Consciously or unconsciously, fear brokers will often project certain characteristics of the Good Parent. They can make us feel the attitudinal equivalent of being patted on the back by a kind authority who tells us that he knows what we have been through, and that he is proud of us for being brave. The scaremonger can act comfortingly omnipotent, as well, implying that, though we are his brave charges, we cannot be expected to be so courageous and strong as he, and that we must always rely on him. He demands that we trust him. He promises that he will never abandon us, and that he will never give up on his goals.

When he adopts a parental persona to secure loyalty, a politician is dealing in very powerful forces, effectively using as leverage the universal religious condemnation of the son or daughter who would betray a parent. If he is a sociopath, or if he is delusional, he may even imply that he is in direct communication with God, who approves his ambitions and plans.

Be on the lookout for a brief ambush by the strange feeling that you would *like* to trust the fear broker. Despite yourself, despite all your good opposing instincts, you may occasionally have a fleeting urge to make this person proud of you. This urge is a glaring warning signal that a perpetrator is present, and though it may be disturbing, such a passing emotion is a normal reaction. You are not responding to the fear politician per se, but to a psychological construct within yourself, one that he is trying like the devil to co-opt.

Step back and file your feeling under "useful warnings." And imagine the emotional impact this politician may be having on those whose subterranean wish for a kind and protective parent figure is less modulated than your own.

6. Fear brokers shame us over sex.

Also like the stereotypical parent, a fear politician wishes to be viewed as the moral and literal rule maker where sexuality is concerned. *Unlike* a good parent, he shames us, and then tries to use this shame to exert control.

Of course, issues pertaining in some way to sexuality—sexual preference, same-sex marriage, birth control, abortion, certain types of medical research, and, most recently, inoculations to prevent cervical cancer—are often discussed politically. Engaging in public debate over such issues does not necessarily constitute fear politics. The fear politician's relationship to these topics is different. He or she uses them manipulatively, as a distraction tactic. When public discussion is moving toward an issue unrelated to fear, thus threatening the politician's ability to control the group, he or she will initiate a conversation about one of the several political topics having to do with sexuality. (In other words, there is a move from using one primal topic, fear, to using another one, sex.) Matters of sexual morality are inherently divisive and highly emotional, and tend to divert us completely from whatever we had been thinking or discussing before. The fear broker adds still more emotional content by highlighting the notion of shame that can attend all things sexual.

In brief, the sixth behavioral earmark of fear brokers has

two parts. First, you will find that a sex-related topic—such as same-sex marriage or the legal status of abortion—has been introduced apropos of nothing, into a very different ongoing discussion that likely had nothing to do with sex. Second, you will hear notes of shame, or maybe even judgments of sin, as they are blended into the changed debate. After these two manipulative actions have been taken, people will be temporarily distracted from their original concerns.

Dragging sex into the discussion, as it were, is reminiscent of the behavior of an abusive spouse whose victim is nearing the point of choosing freedom. Therapy patients who are building the resolve to leave frightening situations (like Kerry in Chapter Six) often relate to me painful stories about being called a whore or a pimp, or some other crude epithet meant to malign someone's sexual and moral nature. It would seem that a verbal assault based on sexuality is an insult of last resort, a distraction technique applied to the captive when the captor is no longer able to evoke sufficient fear. And sometimes the new technique works: the target becomes so fixated on the slur that she or he will stay, at least long enough to try to convince the abuser to rescind it.

In politics, too, the tactic is a tried and true one. For example, Joe McCarthy repeatedly ranted on the Senate floor about a "homosexual underground" that was abetting the "communist conspiracy." This he did despite the fact that, according to some historians, McCarthy's own sexual orientation was toward men. For a while, American business owners became so focused on McCarthy's sexuality-related claims that, often to the detriment of their businesses, they attempted to identify and dismiss all homosexual workers. And in the last nine months of 1950, while the rattled Senate implemented a full-scale investigation of the "homosexual underground," almost six hundred people were fired from government jobs alone. Of course, all of this added up to one of several empty scares that distracted the entire nation from the truly damaging and very real problem of McCarthyism itself.

One wonders what might have happened, how much destruction might have been short-circuited, if we had all clearly understood McCarthy's focus on sexuality to be part of the modus operandi of a fear broker.

7. In a seeming contradiction, fear brokers praise us for being moral and heroic.

You have much to fear, the fear broker assures us—and you are bearing up like the incomparably moral and supremely heroic people the world knows you to be.

In addition to emphasizing the many dangers that surround us, the fear politician regales us with the heady theme of how much more God-fearing, principled, selfless, and altogether admirable we are than everyone else. In various ways, she or he tells us over and again that we, and only we, can take on anything, succeed at anything, and endure anything, in the service of what we know to be right.

Flattery always involves an intent to manipulate. It is not a compliment. The purpose of flattery can be benign (as when someone hopes simply to be liked and accepted), or its aim can be decidedly more sinister—but, in either case, words are being used as a tool in the service of a goal that is not stated. Straightforward, moral leaders almost never use extreme flattery. Supporting the people by reminding them of their genuine strengths and accomplishments is an important aspect of good leadership, but trumpeting their superiority relative to all the other peoples of the world is not.

Listen for what are essentially come-on lines, and know that a person with no hidden agenda would not be speaking them.

8. Fear brokers project personal infallibility.

When times are most frightening, someone who always makes the right decision and who never botches any of his plans is almost irresistibly magnetic. When we have been traumatized, our perceived need for protectors who are infallible is so pressing that we will sometimes override the normal reasoning processes that tell us such people do not exist.

To capitalize on this time-limited form of influence over people, a scaremonger in public office will never admit to mistakes. He or she will be firmly committed to this stance. When you are evaluating a fear politician, look for moments when that individual is asked the direct question *Do you feel you made a mistake?* Invariably, the fear politician's answer will be reducible to one word: *No.*

Various organizations have studied this feature of leadership. One instructive example is the Office of Financial Management at the University of Washington, which reports that those who are willing to admit mistakes belong to a category of leaders who have a genuine "work process focus," a quality that involves recognizing and supporting the team, and an interest in how the job gets done. In contrast, those who lead by using our fears focus solely on achieving and maintaining personal influence—regardless of how this is accomplished—and characteristically, such leaders are unwilling to acknowledge their mistakes.

In his study of the behavior of Americans at work after 9/11,

Jeffrey Kleinberg discovered that the most debilitating instances of "worker's block" occur in organizations led by managers who display this same "infallible" authoritarian style. He found that, especially following a disastrous event, if management lacks the capacity to "self-reflect" accurately, "organizations may focus on inconsequential threats, and fail to perceive significant dynamic forces impeding their restabilization."

9. Fear brokers are secretive, and are certain that other people, too, are keeping dangerous secrets.

In general, paranoia is all about secrecy, one's own secrecy and that suspected of other people. The leader who advances cultural paranoia—who, as history demonstrates, may be moderately to seriously paranoid himself—is typically driven to collect information about other people, while at the same time withholding information about himself and his activities.

In the words of Pol Pot, "Secret work is fundamental."

Look for a leader who is intent on gathering information about his countrymen, though the information may be largely meaningless, and who is unusually reluctant to release facts about himself and those close to him, sometimes for conspicuous reasons and sometimes inexplicably.

10. Fear brokers use language that pulls for primitive affect.

Fear is an ancient emotion. As a facilitator of survival, it is available even to the least advanced of the mammals, and is one of the first emotions to be evident in the human infant. The primitive emotion of fear evokes the famous fight-or-flight reaction, even in an evolutionarily advanced species such as our own. The inclination to flee or to fight often occurs beneath our awareness, and is neurologically associated with primitive behaviors such as ragefulness and violence.

It is relatively easy to arouse fear in people. The emotion is deeply rooted in our past and in our brains, and because of the human facility with language, many words and concepts can evoke moderate levels of fear in people without the near presence of actual danger. One of the most universal of such concepts is that of evil. For centuries, the word *evil*, in all the various languages of the world, has been on the lips of fear brokers and also war makers. It is an overwhelmingly powerful tool. In addition to conjuring fear, the concept of *good versus evil* has the advantages of

> *reassuring the people that they are on the side of good;*
> *creating a division between "us" and "them" that has no gray areas; and*
> *casting as evil all doubters and dissenters.*

Another concept with ancient links to fear is that of *revenge*. Whether or not the word itself is used, a typical fear broker will communicate the primitively appealing notion that the people *should* have revenge, and also that they *will* have revenge, provided they are loyal to him. He may induce still more primitive emotionality by introducing the notion of *cowardice*. Via a series of nonrational twists, the enemies are cowards, and therefore being cowardly is not just shameful—being cowardly means a person is one of the enemies. The scaremonger may deliver these provocative and confusing equations intentionally, or, if he is paranoid, such words and ideas may color his speech spontaneously.

Listen for the frequent use of fear-arousing words such as *evil*, *revenge*, and *cowardice*, and also for menacing words of more recent origin. For example, the word *anthrax* reliably triggers a fear spike in the new-millennium American brain, and may be used unnecessarily by fear politicians to do exactly that. Pay attention, as well, to specific pronoun usage. Moral leaders tend to employ the first person plural, *we*, as in references to what *we* can do to help ourselves. This language promotes responsibility and an encouraging sense that the people are in control. Fear politicians, on the other hand, often use the third person plural, *they*, as in declarations of what *they* (the members of the out-group) have done to hurt us. Use of the third person fosters the pointless project of assigning blame and subtly reinforces a perception that the people are *not* in control.

Laura J. Rediehs, of St. Lawrence University, studies how language affects the process of resolving group conflicts. In an essay entitled "Evil," she writes, "We must always keep in mind that we are in control of our words and concepts: we don't have to let words and concepts control us. When we do place ourselves at the mercy of words and concepts, we are placing ourselves at the mercy of the people who use those words and concepts to control us."

In a democracy, a person displaying some or all of these behaviors would not be well tolerated under ordinary circumstances. Several of the ten characteristics are plainly unattractive and alienating. But, again, the behaviors are unattractive and alienating *under ordinary conditions*. Following a catastrophic national event, such as 9/11 in the United States, conditions are anything but ordinary. The people are traumatized, they long for someone to make them feel secure, and an ancient paranoia switch is once again waiting to snap on. Under these conditions, fear mongers thrive. Their characteristics are so hand in glove with the trauma reaction of the population that their identifying behaviors are scarcely "seen" at all. In short, after we have been thoroughly traumatized, we cannot see the devil.

Since human beings began to live in hierarchical groups—with leaders and followers and group identities—countless societies have undergone debilitating paranoia switches. Usually, even after they have "switched" back to normal, people require decades to understand what happened to them and to see how much destruction was caused by their reiteration of the pattern. After Pearl Harbor, in 1941, the United States did not apologize for its "war hysteria" treatment of the Japanese-Americans until 1988. McCarthyism ended more than half a century ago, yet many of us remain confused and incredulous about the stranglehold McCarthy was able to gain during the Red Scare—that one solitary, embarrassing broker of fear, invisible to us from the end of World War II until 1954.

But in these years after September 11, 2001, we have the opportunity, perhaps unique in the world, to turn a paranoia switch *off* in mid-cycle, to stop attending to those who would retraumatize us, and to recover our home before the decades fly by us. If we are going to meet this historic challenge, we will have to clear our vision and wake our sleeping courage. The final chapter is about our awakening, what it will be like, and what will make it possible.

Free yourself.

—ROSA PARKS

We must guard our nation from terrorist violence and destruction. Nothing could be clearer. There are food supplies, transportation systems, nuclear facilities, chemical plants, landmarks, ports, and cities that need to be secured and protected. But as I write, almost six years after 9/11, the discouraging evidence is that we are not yet adequately guarded at our points of greatest vulnerability, and the worst of the criminals who terrorized and robbed us are still at large. Apparently, our continued high anxiety has not served to propel us into actions that make the nation safer, or that satisfy justice even minimally. Stephen Flynn, a senior fellow with the National Security Studies Program at the Council on Foreign Relations, writes in 2007 that, after the next disaster occurs in the United States, Americans will "painfully discover that our elected and private-sector leaders have been barely going through the motions. Beyond passenger airline security, few meaningful measures have been put into place to construct a credible counterterrorism deterrent at home or to ensure that the emergency plans laid out on paper can actually be carried out in reality." He states that, at its highest levels, our government "treats homeland security as a decidedly second-rate priority."

In a marriage, it is reasonably expected that one spouse will be loyal to and help the other, especially when the other is vulnerable. When this expectation is not met—or when, as in an abusive relationship, vulnerability is actually exploited—there is a sense of disbelief that can delay protest for a while. Similarly, it is natural for decent, rational people in a free nation to believe that all of their leaders share the commonsense goals that would promote national well-being, especially after a large-scale disaster. Here, the hard-won wisdom of McCarthy victim Arthur Miller bears repeating: "Few of us can easily surrender our belief that society must somehow make sense. The thought that the state has lost its mind and is punishing so many innocent people is intolerable. And so the evidence has to be internally denied."

But now, we have discovered, undeniably, that those who dominate by using fear have ambitions primarily of power and control, goals that are advanced all too easily under the guise of protecting the people, but that have nothing to do with their real needs or with the infrastructures that support and protect their lives. In fact, power ambitions and fear tactics weaken the people, rather than making them stronger or more motivated.

Such exploitative politics have induced us, the American people, to act with less competency and courage than we had a right to expect of ourselves, given our history, our resources, and our founding values.

We will be able to make ourselves safe again only when enough of us remember who we are. And, radiating calm and courage—neurologically, psychologically, and spiritually—you yourself may be the one to turn the tide. Both terrorism and fear politics are directed at the individual, at personal fears, at the reflexive reaction to perceived threat that resides in each separate person's brain and mind. In other words, both terrorism and fear politics are directed at *you*, as an individual. And the way you personally deal with these attempts to influence your mind will make a difference, more powerful than you know, in our recovery as a nation. Just as fear gallops through a group of people like a strong-willed horse—so does calm.

To emphasize—terrorism and fear tactics are meant to affect individuals. Personalized fear is far more overpowering than is fear from a distance, or fear in the abstract, and substantially limits our inclination to safeguard the country as a whole. It is impossible to picture the plight of a whole nation in any truly affecting way. Instead, we picture ourselves in the feared situation; we imagine our own families, our own friends, our own streets and subways and schools. After Pearl Harbor, when Secretary of the Navy Frank Knox claimed, for his own face-saving reasons, that the Japanese communities in Hawaii were treacherous, people all over the West Coast were terrified, not of Japanese-Americans in the abstract, but of their own Japanese-American neighbors. At night, they pictured the signal lights of the imaginary saboteurs flickering in the windows of their own towns and cities. Likewise, during the Red Scare, Americans were not terrified of communism as a political force, because it is impossible to have a deep emotional reaction to such an abstraction. Rather, Americans pictured themselves and their families as captives, dressed in rags and shivering in the Siberian snow. Or, if they lived near the coast, they imagined that the Soviets might send submarines full of men who would come ashore on their nearby beaches. Later, we found humor in these unlikely fantasies, and in 1966, a send-up comedy called *The Russians Are Coming, the Russians Are Coming* received an Oscar nomination. But less than a decade before then, the personal threat felt as real as today's weather.

Today, as we once again try to sort out the real from the imaginary, there is bad news about terrorism and good news about terrorism. The bad news concerns our nation and the world as a whole, and the good news has to do with the individual—with you—as you go about your own life. The bad news is this: As an especially heinous category of criminal activity, terrorism has occurred throughout the history of human civilization, and there is no reason to think that, in our lifetime, any policy on the part of any country will end it altogether. It is catastrophically sad, but true, that between the time I write this book, and the time you open it and read this sentence, another act of political terrorism will likely take place somewhere in the world. Before 2001, Americans had not fully realized that the United States was vulnerable to international terrorism. Now, through an agonizing lesson, we have learned that it is.

Still, the extremely good news is—the personal threat of terrorism to *you* is tiny. If you live in the United States, the probability that you personally will be killed by terrorist activity is only somewhat greater than that of your getting hit by space debris, and *overwhelmingly less* than that of your being killed in a car crash. Where your family members are concerned, it would be valid for you to worry less about terrorists and more about whether they are fastening their seat belts. And for you to hamstring your life or radically alter your frame of mind, based on the threat to you of terrorism, is a sad and unnecessary waste. Realistically speaking, international terrorists are less dangerous to you and the people you love than are ill-tempered dogs and slippery bathtubs.

In sum—that there will be additional terrorist attacks is a virtual certainty. As Stephen Flynn states, "It is as inevitable as a hurricane, earthquake, or major flood. And as with those recognized disasters, there are things we can be doing right now to make us a more resilient nation." However, in diametric contrast, the chances that *you* will be injured or killed in a terrorist attack are slim to none.

The astonishing fact is that experts have recognized this crucial distinction almost from the beginning. In 2001, less than three months after the terrorist assault on the United States, *The Washington Post* published an article called "Terrorism and You—The Real Odds," written by the University of Wisconsin professor emeritus Michael L. Rothschild. Professor Rothschild began his analysis by citing the odds of dying in a car accident each year (approximately 1 in 7,000), the odds of dying from cancer in any given year (1 in 600), and those of dying from heart disease in any given year (1 in 400). He then observed, "We have learned to live with these common threats to our health. Yet we have been afraid to return to the malls and the skies." Rothschild's point in 2001 was that, compared with these health statistics, and even in an absolute sense, the threat of terrorism to the individual was truly minuscule, and therefore we should attempt to calm ourselves and resume our lives.

But in 2006, five troubled years after Rothschild's article appeared in the *Post*, the policy analyst John Mueller, of Ohio State University, wrote in *Foreign Affairs* that, far from helping to calm us, American politicians, officials, and journalists had managed to generate "fears of the omnipotent terrorist—reminiscent of those inspired by images of the 20-foot-tall Japanese after Pearl Harbor or the 20-foot-tall Communists at various points in the Cold War." Mueller took pains to impress on the readers of *Foreign Affairs* that this "omnipotent terrorist" had always been, and always would be, nonexistent.

Each of us has his or her own twenty-foot-tall terrorist, or perhaps a plan of escape from him, or a gruesome image of the damage he could do. After the psychological devastation of the attack itself, and the media hype and fear politics that followed, each of us formed at least one especially appalling image or private worst-case scenario, and these pictures still reside in our psyches. These years later, maybe your personal image remains vivid, in the front of your mind, or perhaps you have forgotten and will have to do some digging to find it, but in either case, the thought you formed is still there. My own worst-case scenario no longer races my pulse—in fact, I can hardly believe I was ever panicked enough, even for a day or two, to develop such an irrational and ridiculously unworkable plan—but it is still there, and I can remember it. I imagined that, when the terrorists arrived and blew up the nuclear power plant that stands about forty-five miles from my home in coastal New England, I would gather my family and we would drive northwest, away from the population centers of Boston and New York City, and not stop until we got to the Green Mountains in Vermont, where the air would be free of radiation, and we could hide.

Back in my right mind, I realize that this plan involved—among many other illogical elements—an escape to a location that would have been no more or less secure than my starting place. But the essence of this nightmare scenario, the whole point, was that *home* was not safe. Because of the terrorists, I was about to lose my home. I suspect that many of our dark imaginings about terrorism reflect this particular fear.

Your own worst-case scenario may be similar to mine, or it may be very different. Perhaps, like me, you thought about a plan of escape, or instead, maybe you pictured an inescapable threat, what it would feel like to die of smallpox, or how you would react if you saw a suicide bomber on the subway. When we are terrified, our minds can be mercilessly creative. But whatever your horrific picture, I can tell you that it is not real, it was never real, it was planted in your mind by fear and by power-hungry fear brokers, and right now is the time to get rid of it. If you were my patient, I might ask you to write a description of your image on a sheet of paper, in as much detail as you could remember, and then to tear the paper into little pieces and ceremoniously toss the pieces into the garbage. I might even suggest that you light a match and burn them. Deal the terrorists and the fear mongers a final defeat—cleanse your mind of the implanted image, like you would purge yourself of a poison.

If the image will not go away, talk to yourself. Remind yourself that the idea is not coming from you; it is merely a thought you were conditioned to have, by terrorists and other people who do not deserve a place in your mind.

Shove the image. Glare it down. Inform it that you will not give in, that you are going ahead with your day, and your life.

If the notion comes back, use a technique a recovering trauma patient might use to conquer an obsessive thought: postpone it. Tell yourself that you are going to put the image away and worry about it later—in two hours, or just before dinner tonight, or while you are brushing your teeth after breakfast. Do not allow the image to decide when it will interrupt you. Take back your power a little at a time.

Do not let yourself be ambushed. If the thought tends to come at a particular time of day, or in the context of certain activities, use this information against it. *Expect* the thought and be ready to deal with it, to postpone it or to command it to leave. Or prepare to debate with it, argue it down, using the reasoning of a calmer person whom you trust, or the information you have read in this book. Quote statistics.

Make fun of the image. If you enjoy irony, yell, *The Russians are coming! The Russians are coming!*

Support other people who are getting rid of their own anxious thoughts, and ask them to support you. Remind each other of who you are, of how you used to think and act. Remember that all of you once approached life with less trepidation, that you had the heart to put yourselves out into the world and to pursue ideas that were truly your own. Help yourself and those you love rout out the monstrous images and thoughts implanted by terrorists and thieves. Switch back to your courage.

And listen to the wisdom of our children. In September 2006, the BBC interviewed students who had been with President George W. Bush at Emma Booker Elementary School, in Sarasota, Florida, on the morning of September 11, 2001.

Five years after the disaster, the children had strong opinions, of
course. Most of them predicted that they would always remember that day, that they would tell their own grandchildren about
it. Still, their collective attitude is represented well by a fourteen-
year-old boy who had been nine at the time: "I don't think that
I should have to be scared just walking around. I shouldn't have
to be scared of what's going to happen to me."

COURAGE

I never had to evacuate to the Green Mountains, and I feel sure
you never had to deploy whatever survivalist plans you had
imagined. Still, our national home has changed in ways that are
frightening. The changes were gradual, incremental, hard to detect while they were happening, but in time, some of them
gained a self-sustaining critical mass. As one example—how did
it happen that torture is now practiced under the auspices of the
United States, in our name? Many of us wonder about this, but
we feel too intimidated to protest, and we do not understand
how our policy devolved to such an unthinkable standard in the
first place.

While the American people were busy being terrified, the
official definition of acceptable interrogation procedures changed
quietly, one small step at a time, until everyone involved was effectively desensitized to the commission of torture. Psychologists
refer to the process of incrementally reducing a person's emotional response as *systematic desensitization,* and when used as a
treatment for a debilitating phobic response, the process can be
helpful. A behavior therapist might treat a snake phobia, for ex-

ample, by showing the patient first a picture of a snake, then a toy snake in a cage, then a toy snake outside the cage, and after many such small approaches to the real thing, finally an actual snake. The patient's aversion would lessen one manageable bit at a time, as opposed to the patient's running out the door screaming should the therapist produce a real snake on the first day. Unfortunately, when the goal is less humane, desensitization gets turned on its ear, and begins to resemble the old saw about the easiest way to boil a frog: raise the heat under the pot one degree at a time, and the frog will not try to leap out. In this instance, the frog represents the American people, along with their traditional ideals and values.

In *The Abu Ghraib Investigations: The Official Reports of the Independent Panel and the Pentagon*, editor Steven Strasser presents a table summarizing the changes distributed over two and a half years in U.S. government–approved interrogation techniques, specifically at Guantánamo Bay. He observes that the equivocal techniques employed under the relatively controlled conditions at Guantánamo Bay, Cuba, were even more loosely interpreted when they "migrated" to Abu Ghraib, in Iraq. The table progresses gradually through thirty-seven procedures, from those that are least alarming in the public mind, to those that are most alarming. It reads like any protocol I have ever seen for systematic desensitization, except ambiguously worded, and from hell.

In January 2002, our approved interrogation procedures included, among other techniques, the following:

Direct questioning
Establish your identity
Repetition approach

Rapid fire
Change of scene

Eleven months later, on December 2, 2002, the United States Secretary of Defense approved the following additional procedures, among a number of others:

Deception
Stress positions
Isolation for up to 30 days
Deprivation of light/auditory stimuli
Hooding
Removal of all comfort items, including religious items
Removal of clothing
Exploiting individual phobias, e.g., dogs
Mild, non-injurious physical contact

And on April 16, 2003, in a memo, the Secretary of Defense added a few more procedures to the approved list. After "mild, non-injurious physical contact," these ambiguously described techniques included the following:

Mutt and Jeff
Sleep adjustment
Environmental manipulation

What do these terms mean specifically? This was and is anybody's guess. We know that "Mutt and Jeff" is a reference to the "good cop / bad cop" technique many of us have seen portrayed in television police dramas. But its limitations are not specified, and most of the other authorized techniques are even muddier. In March 2007, Tony Lagouranis, a former U.S. Army interrogator previously stationed in Mosul and at Abu Ghraib, and coauthor of *Fear Up Harsh: An Army Interrogator's Dark Journey Through Iraq*, sent a message to the members of Human Rights First. He wrote that, because the instructions they had received were so ambiguous, the junior soldiers he worked with had turned to television for specific ideas. According to Lagouranis, his unit—using TV as a source of information—staged mock executions and mock drownings, exposed detainees to extremes of hot and cold, and threatened to rape detainees' wives. With no one providing clear guidance to the young soldiers, who were under extraordinary pressure to get information, these approaches evidently managed to find their way into the amorphous categories of "deception," "environmental manipulation," and "exploiting individual phobias."

Gradually, step by scarcely noticed step, the United States approved torture, both psychological and physical. And by the time this had been accomplished, the people of the United States were desensitized to all but actual photographs: American soldiers at Abu Ghraib in the fall of 2003, laughing and pointing at naked prisoners; a terrified man in the corner of a plywood room, cringing from the fangs of a large dog restrained only inches from his neck; and a hooded man with wires creeping under his poncho, standing on a box in an attitude of crucifixion. Suddenly roused from our desensitized slumber, we were sickened, and the photograph of the wired and hooded man, revealed to us in the spring of 2004, soon joined the flaming Twin Towers as an image permanently seared into the American psyche.

When used by a therapist, desensitization is intended to help a willing patient conquer her reflexive emotional reactions, so that she can think and act for herself. When it occurs in the context of fear politics, desensitization reduces our normal emotional reactions to the point of numbness, establishing a greatly lowered probability that we will think or act at all. While we have been encouraged to remain in a panic over a terrorist threat less menacing to American individuals than driving their cars, we have been slowly desensitized to the idea of torturing human beings, and to other human rights violations that normally would cause many Americans to howl in protest—and to the invisible erosion of journalism free of political influence, the loss of some of our own civil rights, and the perilous neglect of our public health infrastructure. Over time, we have been made nearly insensate to a blatant genocide in central Africa, to the bleak plight—still—of our own countrymen on the Gulf Coast after Hurricane Katrina, and to global environmental decline in general. In addition, gradually, one small missed chance at a time, we have put many of our private goals and dreams on hold. Uncounted American lives have been placed in a numbing limbo, because when people are frightened for themselves, they do not often take risks, not even carefully considered risks that could lead to advances in their work, or the fulfillment of personal dreams.

If human rights or other sociopolitical issues have been of special significance to you in times past, I recommend that you once again embrace your conscience and speak up, starting now, in whatever way seems appropriate to you—as part of your recovery from the now chronic effects of our national trauma. If you have delayed a meaningful step in your personal life, I suggest that you gather your determination and resume pursuing your goals right away—again, as a way to heal yourself from the bit-by-bit theft of your courage. I would make such recommendations to a therapy patient recovering from the damage inflicted by individual trauma, as well. Healing is nearly completed when a victim can reclaim her courage and realign her choices with the dreams and values she has always cherished. We can recover from fear when we are able to remember who we are and always have been, and put that knowledge into action.

When we are able to remember ourselves, we can enact ideas and projects aimed at preserving our nation in ways that match our values. Homeland security expert Stephen Flynn reports that few leaders in Washington are asking whether, for example, "a tax dollar that is now being spent to buy a new stealth jet fighter might be better used as a tax incentive to nudge a domestic oil refinery into converting to safer chemicals. Nor is anyone questioning whether we would be better off investing more money on community policing than building a futuristic navy destroyer." We, the people, must ask these sorts of questions ourselves, and insist that the answers be rationally and systematically implemented. And noting that, by virtue of their personalities, Americans have always risen to a challenge, Flynn reminds us, "Building a resilient society is not about caving in to our fears."

In a self-reproachful play called *Struggle Till Dawn*, released after the World War II victory over fascism, the Italian playwright Ugo Betti wrote, "This free will business is a bit terrifying anyway. It's almost pleasanter to obey, and make the most of it." Betti was right. Freedom is frightening, and hard. It requires us to be brave and to remain in charge of our own minds. The opposite of the individual who craves paranoia-evoking authoritarian leaders after a disaster is the individual who has the courage to think for him- or herself. And the continued health of a democracy—rule by the people—unavoidably *requires* that a sufficient number of people think for themselves. (Imagine trying to sustain a democratic form of government in a herd of sheep.) Chronic fear, with its yearning for authoritarian rule, directly opposes our founding ideals, just as our founding ideals are in direct opposition to chronic fear. We can have one or the other, but not both at the same time, at least not for long. Our level of anxiety is not merely a matter of our personal discomfort. Our continued fear has large social and political implications. And healing from it is more than an individual mental health objective—it is a national mission. Striving to be calmer, more aware, and more rational is, arguably, a patriotic act.

If fear holds a democratic nation in thrall in the long term, causing the greater portion of its citizens to avoid thinking for themselves indefinitely, the best psychological prediction is that democracy will decline and eventually die. In the case of the United States, this would mean that the terrorists had won completely, just as tiny pellets of gravel hitting a windshield will, with time, shatter the entire pane of glass. But there is another possible outcome of the terror we have endured, a bold victory over fear that would be unique in human history. The paranoia switch is an ancient story, all over the world; however, actively defying the transformation—switching back—is an attempt that has never been made. When nations, including our own, have recovered in the past, the return to normal has been merely a function of time, as the years and decades erased troubling memories. Perhaps the United States, with its founding commitment to the preservation of liberty, can be the first nation to pass another milestone in the development of humanity: maybe we can wake up from our misty nightmare now, and return home deliberately, to our right minds and values.

Our native country feels changed, and in a manner of speaking, we are homesick. We can wait for the years to go by, until our paranoia dwindles with the passage of time—along with our memory of the wasteful pattern we repeated—or we can take this opportunity to be the first nation in history actually to win a limbic war. With our ancestors pulling for us, our children counting on us, and an anxious world looking on, we can switch back to the people we have always been. We can break the spell of terror, and go home.

NOTES

Chapter One: Homesick World

9 *a Pew Research Center survey found.* As reported in A. Kaplan, "Anticipated Mental Health Consequences of the Sept. 11 Attacks: What Can We Do Now?" *Psychiatric Times* 18 (2001), no. 11.

9 *And research on national samples.* S. Galea, J. Ahern, H. Resnick, D. Kilpatrick, M. Bucuvalas, J. Gold, and D. Vlahov, "Psychological Sequelae of the September 11 Terrorist Attacks in New York City," *New England Journal of Medicine,* Special Report, 346 (2002), 982–87.

9 *Two months later, a* Los Angeles Times *poll.* As reported in S. Pinkus, "Poll Analysis: Psychological Effects of Sept. 11:

Americans Are Coming to Grips with the Events of Sept. 11 and Their Aftermath," *Los Angeles Times*, December 21, 2001.

10 *Study findings presented at the 2002 Scientific Sessions of the American Heart Association.* As reported in L. Altman, "Dangerous Heart Rhythms Increased After 9/11," *The New York Times*, November 21, 2002.

10 *Supporting this speculation, most post-9/11 studies.* See, for example, W. Schlenger, J. Caddell, L. Ebert, B. Jordan, K. Rourke, D. Wilson, L. Thalji, J. Dennis, J. Fairbank, and R. Kulka, "Psychological Reactions to Terrorist Attacks: Findings from the National Study of Americans' Reactions to September 11," *Journal of the American Medical Association* 288 (2002), 581–88.

10 *the babies of those mothers who had developed post-traumatic stress disorder.* R. Yehuda, S. Engel, S. Brand, J. Seckl, S. Marcus, and G. Berkowitz, "Transgenerational Effects of Posttraumatic Stress Disorder in Babies of Mothers Exposed to the World Trade Center Attacks During Pregnancy," *The Journal of Clinical Endocrinology and Metabolism* 90 (2005), 4115–18.

11 *the grown children of World War II Holocaust survivors.* R. Yehuda, L. Bierer, J. Schmeidler, D. Aferiat, I. Breslau, S. Dolan, "Low Cortisol and Risk for PTSD in Adult Offspring of Holocaust Survivors," *American Journal of Psychiatry* 157 (2000), 1252–59.

12 *In a letter to the 110th Precinct Community Council.* As quoted in M. Efthimiades, "Big Drop in Crime for 110th Precinct: Despite Rescue Effort, Police Are Still on the Job," *Times Newsweekly*, September 27, 2001.

14 *To use recognizable examples from the psychiatrist and writer Thomas Lewis.* T. Lewis, F. Amini, and R. Lannon, *A General Theory of Love* (New York: Vintage, 2001), p. 64.

Chapter Two: How Terrorism Works

22 *As but one especially fierce illustration.* Quoted in J. Glazov, "New Glory," *Front Page Magazine*, September 7, 2005.

27 *In a white paper on terrorism, released in 2005.* R. Yehuda and S. Hyman, "The Impact of Terrorism on Brain and Behavior: What We Know and What We Need to Know," *Neuropsychopharmacology* 30 (2005), 1773–80.

27 *In line with my definition, the Israeli scholar Boaz Ganor.* B. Ganor, "Terrorism as a Strategy of Psychological Warfare," in Y. Danieli, D. Brom, and J. Sills (eds.), *The Trauma of Terrorism: Sharing Knowledge and Shared Care, An International Handbook* (Binghamton, NY: Haworth Press, 2005), p. 38. For a detailed account of the many definitions of terrorism, see C. Martin, "The Nature of the Beast," *Understanding Terrorism: Challenges, Perspectives, and Issues*, 2nd ed. (Thousand Oaks, CA: Sage Publications, 2006).

28 *the military analyst Paul R. Pillar.* P. Pillar, *Terrorism and U.S. Foreign Policy* (Washington, DC: Brookings Institution Press, 2001), p. 219.

28 *In 2004, applied health scientists at Indiana University.* M. Torabi and D. Seo, "National Study of Behavioral and Life Changes Since September 11," *Health, Education and Behavior* 31 (2004), 179–92.

30 *the lasting effects of terrorism on the American workforce.* J. Kleinberg, "On the Job After 9/11: Looking at Worker's Block Through a Group Lens," *Group Analysis* 38 (2005), 203–18.

32 *I had read the chastening* Washington Post *article.* M. Rothschild, "Terrorism and You—the Real Odds," *The Washington Post*, November 25, 2001.

35 *researchers contacted a representative sample of adult Londoners.* G. Rubin, C. Brewin, N. Greenberg, J. Simpson, and S. Wessely, "Psychological and Behavioural Reactions to the Bomb-

ings in London on 7 July 2005: Cross Sectional Survey of a Representative Sample of Londoners," *British Medical Journal* 331 (2005), 606.

35 *For example, the BBC world affairs editor, John Simpson, observed.* J. Simpson, "London Bombs Need Calm Response," *BBC News*, August 31, 2005.

36 *Israeli society provides another significant illustration of relative equanimity.* A. Bleich, M. Gelkopf, and Z. Solomon, "Exposure to Terrorism, Stress-Related Mental Health Symptoms, and Coping Behaviors Among a Nationally Representative Sample in Israel," *Journal of the American Medical Association* 290 (2003), 612–20; P. Roy-Byrne, "Effects of Terror and Violence Vary by Culture," *Journal Watch Psychiatry*, October 8, 2003.

36 *The Israeli psychologists.* Y. Klar, D. Zakay, and K. Sharvit, " 'If I Don't Get Blown Up . . .': Realism in Face of Terrorism in an Israeli Nationwide Sample," *Risk, Decision and Policy* 7 (2002), 203–19.

43 *neuropsychologists think that a part of the brain, the infralimbic area.* For the report of an interesting animal study concerning safety signals and the prefrontal cortex, see M. Milad and G. Quirk, "Neurons in Medial Prefrontal Cortex Signal Memory for Fear Extinction," *Nature* 420 (2002), 70–74.

Chapter Three: The Day They Captured Cat Stevens

45 *Gavin de Becker.* G. de Becker, *The Gift of Fear: Survival Signals That Protect Us from Violence* (Boston: Little, Brown, 1997).

56 *For the last twenty-five years, my therapy patients.* M. Stout, *The Myth of Sanity: Divided Consciousness and the Promise of Awareness* (New York: Viking, 2001). Also, see *The Myth of Sanity* for a detailed discussion of the neuropsychological effects of trauma on memory and personality.

59   *In his review of the documentary film.* M. Seitz, "Film," *New York Press* 15:36 (2002).

62   *some forms of traumatic stress are even more psychologically toxic.* For a discussion of the research on the relative impact of various forms of traumatic stress, see A. McFarlane and G. de Giro-lamo, "The Nature of Traumatic Stressors and the Epidemiology of Posttraumatic Reactions," in B. van der Kolk, A. McFarlane, and L. Weisaeth (eds.), *Traumatic Stress: The Effects of Overwhelming Experience on Mind, Body, and Society* (New York: Guilford Press, 1996). See also E. Deykin and S. Buka, "The Prevalence and Risk Factors for Posttraumatic Stress Disorder Among Chemically Dependent Adolescents," *American Journal of Psychiatry* 154 (1997), 752–57; R. Giacona, H. Reinherz, A. Silverman, B. Pakiz, A. Frost, and E. Cohen, "Traumas and PTSD in a Community Population of Older Adolescents," *Journal of the American Academy of Child and Adolescent Psychiatry* 34 (1995), 1369–80; and K. Kilpatrick and L. Williams, "Posttraumatic Stress Disorder in Child Witnesses to Domestic Violence," *Journal of Orthopsychiatry* 67 (1997), 639–44.

Chapter Four: Fearing As One

75   *the first psychological definition of conscience.* M. Stout, *The Sociopath Next Door: The Ruthless Versus the Rest of Us* (New York: Broadway Books, 2005), pp. 22–26.

76   *electrical stimulation of limbic sectors evoked visceral sensations and emotions.* E. Halgren, "Mental Phenomena Induced by Stimulation in the Limbic System," *Human Neurobiology* 1 (1982), 251–60.

76   *employing functional magnetic resonance imaging.* K. Phan, D. Fitzgerald, K. Gao, G. Moore, M. Tancer, and S. Posse, "Real-Time fMRI of Cortico-Limbic Brain Activity During Emotional Processing," *Neuroreport* 15 (2004), 527–32.

78   *Thomas Lewis, Fari Amini, and Richard Lannon.* T. Lewis,
      F. Amini, and R. Lannon, *A General Theory of Love* (New
      York: Vintage, 2001), p. 63.

79   *Allan Schore.* A. Schore, *Affect Regulation and the Repair of the
      Self* (New York: Norton, 2003), p. 48.

79   *perceived by another person's amygdala.* L. Pessoa, S. Japee, and
      L. Ungerleider, "Visual Awareness and the Detection of Fear-
      ful Faces," *Emotion* 5 (2005), 243–47.

79   *Ross Buck.* R. Buck, "The Neuropsychology of Communica-
      tion: Spontaneous and Symbolic Aspects," *Journal of Pragmatics*
      22 (1994), 265–78.

80   *"literally a biological unit."* Ibid., p. 266.

81   *the cerebrospinal fluid of grown bonnet macaques.* J. Coplan,
      R. Trost, M. Owens, T. Cooper, J. Gorman, C. Nemeroff,
      and L. Rosenblum, "Cerebrospinal Fluid Concentrations
      of Somatostatin and Biogenic Amines in Grown Primates
      Reared by Mothers Exposed to Manipulated Foraging Con-
      ditions," *Archives of General Psychiatry* 55 (1998), 473–77.

82   *mother is asked to freeze her face for a moment.* T. Brazelton,
      E. Tronick, L. Adamson, H. Als, and S. Wise, "Early Mother-
      Infant Reciprocity," *Ciba Foundation Symposium* 33 (1975),
      137–54.

82   *Sigmund Freud told his students.* S. Freud, "Recommendations
      to Physicians Practicing Psycho-analysis," in J. Strachey (ed.
      and trans.), *Standard Edition of the Complete Psychological Works
      of Sigmund Freud,* vol. 12 (London: Hogarth Press, 1958),
      p. 115. (Original work published 1912.)

Chapter Five: The Limbic Wars

95   *the largest authoritarian hate group in the history of the United
      States.* For comprehensive information on the history and ac-
      tivities of the Ku Klux Klan, see M. Newton, *The Ku Klux*

Klan: History, Organization, Language, Influence and Activities of America's Most Notorious Secret Society (Jefferson, NC: McFarland, 2006).

97   *Knox's move to scapegoat the Japanese-Americans.* See R. Daniels, *Concentration Camps, North America: Japanese in the United States and Canada During World War II* (Malabar, FL: Krieger, 1993).

101 *the political pressures on FDR.* See G. Robinson, *By Order of the President: FDR and the Internment of Japanese Americans* (Cambridge, MA: Harvard University Press, 2003).

102 *"a dignified group of people."* C. Brauchli, "History Recapitulates: Guantanamo and the Japanese Internment Camps," *CounterPunch,* July 21, 2003.

106 *Richard Fried has noted extreme instances of our irrationality during McCarthy's reign.* R. Fried, *Nightmare in Red: The McCarthy Era in Perspective* (New York: Oxford University Press, 1991).

108 *Miller wrote in an article for* The New Yorker. A. Miller, "Why I Wrote *The Crucible,*" *The New Yorker,* October 21, 1996.

113 *"Few of us can easily surrender our belief."* Ibid.

Chapter Six: The Terrorist in the Closet

120 *Nearly one third of American women.* K. Collins, C. Schoen, S. Joseph, et al., "Health Concerns Across a Woman's Lifespan: The Commonwealth Fund 1998 Survey of Women's Health," *The Commonwealth Fund Report,* May 1999.

120 *Similarly, around the world, at least one in every three women.* L. Heise, M. Ellsberg, and M. Gottemoeller, "Ending Violence Against Women," *Population Reports,* Series L (1999), no. 11.

120 *On average, more than three American women.* C. Rennison, "Intimate Partner Violence, 1993–2001," *Bureau of Justice Statistics Crime Data Brief,* February 2003.

120   *for women who are pregnant.* A. Nannini, J. Weiss, R. Goldstein, and S. Fogerty, "Pregnancy-Associated Mortality at the End of the Twentieth Century: Massachusetts, 1990–1999," *Journal of the American Medical Women's Association* 57 (2002), 140–43.

120   *Approximately 15 percent of partner-violence victims are men.* C. Rennison, "Intimate Partner Violence," 1993–2001.

131   *Each year, in the United States alone.* J. Miller, "Domestic Violence Fact Sheet" (Woodinville, WA: At Health, 2006).

136   *a scholarly analysis of the personalities of 377 leaders.* A. Ludwig, *King of the Mountain: The Nature of Political Leadership* (Lexington, KY: University Press of Kentucky, 2002).

142   *nuclear annihilation.* J. Schell, *The Fate of the Earth* (New York: Viking, 1982).

Chapter Seven: Fear and the Soul of a Nation

148   *the University of Pennsylvania political scientist Diana Mutz.* See, for example, D. Mutz and B. Reeves, "The New Videomalaise: Effects of Televised Incivility on Political Trust," *American Political Science Review* 99 (2005), 1–15.

152   *the ratio of inborn effects to environmental influences.* For more information concerning this ratio in personality features, and seminal research, see L. Eaves, H. Eysenck, and N. Martin, *Genes, Culture and Personality* (New York: Academic Press, 1989).

153   *the political attitudes of a large sample of twins.* J. Alford, C. Funk, and J. Hibbing, "Are Political Orientations Genetically Transmitted?" *American Political Science Review* 99 (2005), 153–67.

153   Wilson-Patterson Attitude Inventory. G. Wilson and G. Patterson, "A New Measure of Conservatism," *British Journal of Social and Clinical Psychology* 7 (1968), 264–69.

161   *Geoffrey R. Stone.* G. Stone, *Perilous Times: Free Speech in Wartime* (New York: Norton, 2004), p. 5.

162 *warning from Justice Robert H. Jackson.* R. Jackson, *Wartime Security and Liberty Under Law* (Buffalo, NY: University of Buffalo School of Law, 1951).

164 *Ed Bacon, the rector of the All Saints Episcopal Church.* ABC News, "Some See 'Moral Values' Hijacked by the Right," May 29, 2005.

164 *"Many of us feel that our faith has been stolen."* J. Wallis, *God's Politics: Why the Right Gets It Wrong and the Left Doesn't Get It* (San Francisco: HarperSanFrancisco, 2005), p. 3.

165 *the most precipitous drop in theater attendance.* M. Hostetter, "Flailing After 9/11," *Gotham Gazette*, December 2001.

165 *In 2003, arts agencies.* J. Lowell, *State Arts Agencies in Search of Themselves, 1965–2003* (Santa Monica: Rand Research in the Arts, 2004).

165 *gun sales increased.* E. Ashcraft, "Gun Sales Up Nationally Since Sept. 11," *El Independiente* (South Tucson), November 2001.

165 *in the wake of Hurricane Katrina.* For interesting commentary on gun sales and Hurricane Katrina, see M. Ayoob, "Katrina's Lessons: Selling the Right Stuff," *Shooting Industry*, November 2005.

166 *the University of North Carolina's fall reading list for freshmen.* E. Hoover, "North Carolina Campus Holds Seminars on Book About the Koran amid Claims of Victory for Academic Freedom," *The Chronicle of Higher Education*, August 20, 2002.

166 *took to task a professor of religious studies at Pomona College.* J. Martin and A. Neal, *Defending Civilization: How Our Universities Are Failing America and What Can Be Done About It* (Washington, D.C.: American Council of Trustees and Alumni, 2002).

166 *The U.S. Department of Education.* J. Margulies, "Bush Administration Allows Research-Protections Panel to Expire," *The Chronicle of Higher Education*, September 18, 2002.

166 *The Office of Homeland Security revealed.* See E. Skolnikoff, "Research Universities and National Security: Can Traditional Values Survive?" in A. Teich, S. Nelson, and S. Lita (eds.), *Science and Technology in a Vulnerable World*, Washington, D.C.: American Association for the Advancement of Science; and M. Burgan, "Academic Freedom in a World of Moral Crises," *The Chronicle of Higher Education*, September 6, 2002, p. B20.

167 *Federal reports in 2006 disclosed.* D. Barrett, "6 of 75 Cities Get Top Disaster Rating," Associated Press, January 2, 2007.

Chapter Eight: Why We Cannot See the Devil

173 *I used this definition in my discussion of* sociopathy. M. Stout, *The Sociopath Next Door: The Ruthless Versus the Rest of Us* (New York: Broadway Books, 2005).

174 *many of history's most genocidal tyrants.* For a discussion of this topic, see R. Robins and J. Post, *Political Paranoia: The Psychopolitics of Hatred* (New Haven: Yale University Press, 1997).

180 *McCarthy's sexuality-related claims.* See D. Johnson, *The Lavender Scare: The Cold War Persecution of Gays and Lesbians in the Federal Government* (Chicago: University of Chicago Press, 2004).

182 *"work process focus."* University of Washington Office of Financial Management, "Staff and Leader Qualities," University of Washington, June 25, 2006.

182 *In his study of the behavior of Americans at work.* J. Kleinberg, "On the Job After 9/11: Looking at Worker's Block Through a Group Lens," *Group Analysis* 38 (2005), 203–18.

183 *In the words of Pol Pot.* As quoted in D. Chandler, *Brother Number One: A Political Biography of Pol Pot* (Boulder, CO: Westview Press, 1999), p. 150.

185 *In an essay entitled "Evil."* L. Rediehs, "Evil," in J. Collins and

R. Glover (eds.), *Collateral Language: A User's Guide to America's New War* (New York: New York University Press, 2002), pp. 77–78.

Chapter Nine: Homeland Security

187 *Stephen Flynn.* S. Flynn, *The Edge of Disaster: Rebuilding a Resilient Nation* (New York: Random House in cooperation with the Council on Foreign Relations, 2007).

191 *"as inevitable as a hurricane."* Ibid., p. 37.

191 *less than three months after.* M. Rothschild, "Terrorism and You—The Real Odds," *The Washington Post*, November 25, 2001.

192 *"fears of the omnipotent terrorist."* J. Mueller, "Is There Still a Terrorist Threat?" *Foreign Affairs*, September/October 2006.

194 *In September 2006, the BBC interviewed students.* "School Kids Looked Bush in the Eye on 9/11," *BBC News*, September 10, 2006.

196 *The table progresses gradually.* S. Strasser (ed.), *The Abu Ghraib Investigations: The Official Reports of the Independent Panel and the Pentagon* (New York: PublicAffairs, 2004), Appendix C.

198 *the junior soldiers he worked with had turned to television.* T. Lagouranis and A. Mikaelian, *Fear Up Harsh: An Army Interrogator's Dark Journey Through Iraq* (New York: New American Library, 2007).

200 *"a tax dollar that is now being spent."* S. Flynn, *The Edge of Disaster*, p. 169.

200 *"Building a resilient society."* Ibid., p. 180.

ACKNOWLEDGMENTS

Without my trusted friend and literary agent, Susan Lee Cohen, this book would not be. I think I may never figure out which amazes me more about Susan, her rare intellect or her beautiful heart, and I know I will never be able to thank her enough for the difference she has made in my life.

It is my pleasure to thank my editor and publisher, Sarah Crichton, whose loveliness and creativity actually do match the legend. Working with Sarah has been a blessing and a revelation, and if I had three wishes, one would be to know her for a very long time.

I would like to thank all at Farrar, Straus and Giroux who

have helped to make this book. The people at FSG shine with a special light, I have decided. I am grateful in particular to Rose Lichter-Marck, my calm and organized rescuer on more than one occasion.

I dedicate this book to Amanda Kielley, and I want to thank her again here. As a writer, I am grateful for the invaluable ideas she has shared with me. As a human being, I am grateful to the universe for sharing with me a daughter of such beauty, wisdom, and integrity.

As always, I am grateful to my extraordinary and courageous parents, Eva Deaton Stout and Adrian Phillip Stout, and to my treasured brother and lifelong hero, Steve Stout. Also, I would like to take this opportunity to record a joyful welcome to the youngest member of our family, Steve's excruciatingly charming new son, Sam Stout.

For their commentary and their support while I was writing, I thank Howard Kielley, Amy Seabrook, Lucretia Seabrook, Diane Wemyss, and Monica Wemyss.

And I would like to acknowledge the generosity and bravery of the trauma patients who, with the aim of helping others, allowed me to use their stories here. They are anonymous in the book, but in my heart, I remember and admire each one.

To all these remarkable people, and to every one of my wonderful readers, a thousand thanks and then a thousand more.

INDEX

abortion rights, 179, 180
absolutist/contextualist continuum, 155–56, 157
*Abu Ghraib Investigations: The
 Official Reports of the Independent Panel and the Pentagon*,
 196
abusive situations: childhood
 abuse, 56, 121, 149–50; domestic abuse, *see* domestic
 abuse; secrecy and, 117–21,
 134, 146–47, 183; sexual
 abuse, 114
accidents, traumatic stress caused

by, 62; case study, 63–68, 77,
 85–88, 91–92
Adventures of Robin Hood, The
 (Pyle), 106–107
Alford, John, 153–57
American Civil War, 94, 110,
 112, 147
American College of Neuropsy-
 chopharmacology, 27
American Council of Trustees
 and Alumni (ACTA), 166
American Heart Association, 10
American Political Science Review,
 153

American Psychiatric Associa-
    tion, 31
Amini, Fari, 78
amygdala, 51, 52, 72
anthrax, 12, 185
anxiety: anti-anxiety techniques,
    85; The Walking-Around
    Anxiety Test, 16–19; *see also*
    fear
arts: after 9/11, 165; in cultural
    regression stage of limbic war,
    113; McCarthyism and, 107–
    108, 112, 165
Ashcroft, John, 160–61
authoritarian leaders, 111, 201;
    see also fear brokers

Bacon, Ed, 164
battered spouse syndrome, 122,
    159; case study, 122–33
BBC, 194–95
Bernstein, Leonard, 107
Betti, Ugo, 200
bioterrorism, 10, 89
brain: limbic system, *see* limbic
    system; nontraumatic and
    traumatic memory and, 51–57
Brauchli, Christopher, 102
Broca, Paul, 72
Buck, Ross, 79, 80
Bush, George W., administration
    of, 119, 194

censorship, 106–107, 118–19,
    161, 165–66
cerebral cortex, 51
Chaplin, Charlie, 107
Cheney, Dick, 12
childhood abuse, 56, 121, 149–
    50
China, Mao's rule of, 135–36
Churchill, Winston, 103
Cincinnati Reds, 106
Civil Disobedience (Thoreau), 107,
    165
civil liberties, 13; after 9/11,
    160–61, 199; balance between
    national security and, 161–63;
    in cultural regression stage of
    limbic war, 113; of Japanese-
    Americans, *see* Japanese-
    Americans, internment of
CNN/*Time* magazine polls, 10
communism, 110; Red Scare and
    McCarthyism, 103–109, 110,
    112, 114, 115, 118, 161–62,
    165, 170–72, 180–81, 186
Communist Party, 105
Conroy, Pat, 150
conscience, human, 75, 173;
    psychological definition of, 75
contextualist/absolutist contin-
    uum, 155–56, 157
contrast effect, 40–42
coping mechanisms, 39
Copland, Aaron, 107

cortisol, 11
courage, 132, 143, 189, 201
cowardice, 184, 185
cowbird politics, 158
Crowe, James, 94
Crucible, The (Miller), 108
cultural regression stage of limbic
    war, 112–13

de Becker, Gavin, 45
Debs, Eugene, 162
democracy, survival of, 201
desensitization, systematic, 195–
    99
dissociative reactions, 9, 56–57
domestic abuse, 120–33, 141,
    159, 180; case study, 122–33
Dryden, John, 3

Eisenhower, Dwight D., 108
emotions: contagion of, *see* lim-
    bic resonance; evolution and
    the mammalian brain, 74; reg-
    ulation of, *see* limbic system
"End Times," 163–64
environmentalists, 163–64, 199
evil versus good, concept of,
    184, 185
"Exposure to Terrorism, Stress-
    Related Mental Health Symp-
    toms, and Coping Behaviors

Among a Nationally Repre-
    sentative Sample in Israel," 36
extroverts, 151–52, 156–57

fallout shelters, 104
Fate of the Earth, The (Schell),
    142
fear, 201; as contagious, *see* lim-
    bic resonance; continuum of
    reactions to, 46–47; evolution
    of capacity for, 45–46; as
    weapon of terrorism, 14, 25,
    26, 28, 34; *see also* trauma
fear brokers: behavioral charac-
    teristics of, 174–86; identify-
    ing contemporary, 172–86;
    parallels in domestic abuse,
    120–35, 159, 180; *Political
    Greatness Scale* (PGS), 136–37;
    political partisanship and,
    147–50, 157–58; resisting,
    111; seeking protection of,
    129–37, 188; stage of limbic
    war, 110–11
fear switch, *see* paranoia switch
*Fear Up Harsh: An Army Inter-
    rogator's Dark Journey Through
    Iraq* (Lagouranis et al.), 198
Federal Bureau of Investigation
    (FBI), 98, 161, 165
Federal Communications Com-
    mission (FCC), 98

fight-or-flight response, 183–84

flashbacks, 55

Flynn, Stephen, 187–88, 191, 200

Foreign Affairs, 192

Freedom of Information Act, 160

free speech, 162, 163; censorship, 106–107, 118–19, 161, 165–66

Freud, Sigmund, 75, 82–83

Fried, Richard, 106

Funk, Carolyn, 153–57

Galatioto, Natale, 12

Ganor, Boaz, 27

God's Politics: Why the Right Gets It Wrong and the Left Doesn't Get It (Wallis), 164

good versus evil, concept of, 184, 185

Göring, Hermann, 91

group trauma stage of limbic war, 109–10

gun control, 157

gun sales after 9/11, 165

habituation, 37–39, 88

Hammett, Dashiell, 107

Hellman, Lillian, 107

Hibbing, John, 153–57

hippocampus, 51, 52, 54, 72

Hollywood blacklist, 107

Holocaust survivors, children of, 11

homeland security, *see* national security

Homeland Security, Department of, 48, 167

homosexuality, 113–14, 163, 180–81

Hoover, J. Edgar, 101

House Un-American Activities Committee (HUAC), 106, 161–62

Hughes, Langston, 107

Human Rights First, 198

Hurricane Katrina, 165, 199

Hyman, Steven, 27

hypnosis, 87–88

hypothalamus, 72

Indiana University, 28–29

infallibility, fear brokers and personal, 182–83

infant and mother, limbic resonance between, 81–82

intersubjectivity, 79

introverts, 151–52, 156–57

Iraq war, 112, 118–19

iron curtain, 103

Islam, Yusuf (Cat Stevens), 47–50, 61

Islamic cultures and individuals, antagonism toward, 30, 35, 146, 163
isolation and secrecy, abusive situations and, 117–21, 134, 146–47, 183
Israel, 36–37

Jackson, Justice Robert H., 162
Japanese-Americans, internment of, 95–102, 110, 112, 162, 186, 189–90
Jones, Calvin, 94
Journal of Clinical Endocrinology and Metabolism, 10

Keen, Sam, 45
Kennedy, John, 94
Kerr, Jeannie, 114
King, Martin Luther, Jr., 145
Klar, Yechiel, 36
Kleinberg, Jeffrey, 30–31, 183
Knox, Frank, 97, 189
Ku Klux Klan (KKK), 94–95, 110, 112

Lagouranis, Tony, 198
Landry, David, 119
Lannon, Richard, 78

leadership, political, *see* fear brokers; politics of fear
Lester, John, 94
Lewis, Thomas, 14, 78
limbic resonance, 10–11, 77–84, 189; case study, 68–72, 84–85; defined, 78; fear and, 14–15; illustration in "lower" primates, 81
limbic system, 6, 14, 72–74; functions of, 73–74; of mammals, 45–46; research on, 75–76
limbic warfare, 93–116, 202; cultural regression, 112–13; fear broker(s), 110–11; group trauma, 109–10; parallels in domestic abuse, 120–35, 159, 180; recognition and backlash, 113–14; regret and forgetting, 114; scapegoatism, 111–12; stages of, 109–14
Lincoln, Abraham, 117
Lippmann, Walter, 98
London subway bombings of 2005, 35
Los Angeles Times, 9, 97–98, 98–101
Ludwig, Arnold M., 136–37

Machiavelli, Niccolò, 93
Mao Tse-tung, 136

McCarthy, Joseph, and Mc-
    Carthyism, 104–109, 110,
    112, 114, 115, 118, 158, 161–
    62, 165, 170–72, 180–81,
    186, 190
McCord, Frank, 94
Melville, Herman, 63
memory: limbic system and,
    see limbic system; nontrau-
    matic, 51–52; traumatic, 52–
    57
Meredith, Burgess, 107
Miller, Arthur, 107–108, 113,
    114, 188
mistakes, admission of, 182–
    83
Mostel, Zero, 107
mother and child, limbic reso-
    nance between, 81–82; case
    study, 68–72, 84–85
Mount Sinai School of Medi-
    cine, 10
Mueller, John, 192
Murrow, Edward R., 21
Muslims, see Islamic cultures and
    individuals
Mutz, Diana, 148
Myth of Sanity, The (Stout), 8

Napoléon I, 93
national security, 13–14; balance
    between civil liberties and,

161–63; changes in, 166–67,
    187–88
National Security Agency, 167
"National Study of Behavioral
    and Life Changes Since Sep-
    tember 11," 28–29
natural disasters ("acts of God"),
    110; traumatic stress caused by,
    62
nature/nurture: personality char-
    acteristics and, 152–53; politi-
    cal orientation and, 153–57
neurotransmitters, 73
New England Journal of Medicine, 9
New Glory: Expanding America's
    Global Supremacy (Peters), 22–
    23
New Yorker, The, 108
New York Times, The, 137–41,
    161
Nobel Peace Laureates, Commit-
    tee of, 48–49
nonverbal expression, limbic res-
    onance and, 79–80
norepinephrine, 6
nuclear weapons, 103–104, 142
nurturing behavior, 74, 76

Odets, Clifford, 107
Office of Homeland Security,
    166
"On the Job After 9/11," 30–31

paranoia switch, 50, 53–55, 60–
61; examples of triggering,
54–55, 56–57; limbic warfare,
see limbic warfare; politics of
fear, *see* politics of fear;
switching back, 201–202;
triggered by successful terrorism, 24–25
paranoid psychosis, 173–74
Parks, Rosa, 187
patriotism, 113, 176, 201
Pearl Harbor, reaction to, 95–
102, 110, 112, 162, 186, 189–
90
Pentagon Papers, 161
perceptual contrast effect, 40
*Perilous Times: Free Speech in
Wartime* (Stone), 161–62
personality characteristics, 150–
52; absolutist/contextualist
continuum, 155–56, 157;
nature/nurture and, 152–53
Peters, Ralph, 22–23
Pew Research Center, 9
Pillar, Paul R., 28
play behavior, 74, 76
Political Greatness Scale (PGS),
136–37
political orientation, genetic
component of, 153–57
political partisanship, 146–50,
157–58
politics of fear, 12, 15, 89–90,

92–116, 189; fear brokers, *see*
fear brokers; internment of
Japanese-Americans, *see*
Japanese-Americans, internment of; Ku Klux Klan, 94–
95, 110, 112; parallels in domestic abuse, 120–35, 159,
180; political partisanship and,
146–50, 157–58; Red Scare
and McCarthyism, 103–109,
110, 112, 114, 115, 118, 165,
170–72, 180–81, 186, 190;
stages of limbic warfare, 109–
14
Pol Pot, 183
Pomona College, 166
postponing technique, 194
post-traumatic stress disorder
(PTSD), 9, 10–11, 31, 54–56,
88, 92; symptoms of, 55–56
Prince, The (Machiavelli), 93
Prince of Tides, The (Conroy), 150
privacy rights, after 9/11, 160,
163
prosodic stimuli, 79, 80

Reagan, Ronald, 102
recognition and backlash stage of
limbic war, 113–14
Rediehs, Laura J., 185
Red Scare, *see* communism, Red
Scare and McCarthyism

Reed, Richard, 94

regret and forgetting stage of limbic war, 114

religious leaders, after 9/11, 163–64

retraumatizing the affected party, 111, 132; courage not to be retraumatized, 132, 143, 189, 201

revenge, 184, 185; cultural regression and, 112–13

Robeson, Paul, 107

Robinson, Edward G., 107

Robinson, Greg, 101

Roosevelt, Franklin D., 97, 101, 102

Rosenberg, Julius and Ethel, 104

Rothschild, Michael L., 32, 191–92

Russians Are Coming, The Russians Are Coming, The, 190

safety signals, psychological, 43–44, 47

same-sex marriage, 157–58, 179, 180

scapegoatism stage of limbic war, 111–12

Schell, Jonathan, 142

Schore, Allan, 79, 82

scientific inquiry, freedom of, 166

Seattle Times, 119

secrecy and isolation, abusive situations and, 117–21, 134, 146–47, 183

security: looking to fear brokers for protection, 129–37, 188; national, see national security

security, sense of, 184, 185

Sedition Act of 1798, 161

Seeger, Pete, 107

Seitz, Matt Zoller, 59–60

September 11, 2001: behavioral changes after, 29–31, 58; children, wisdom of, 194–95; con artists and, 11–12, 170; contrast effect and, 40–42; interrogation procedures after, 195–99; life before, memories of, 4–5, 159; long-term psychological effects of, 6–8, 9–11, 28–34, 50, 57–61, 88–89; media coverage of, 10, 59–60, 137–41; memories of, 4; political partisanship after, 147–50; scapegoatism after, 112; solidarity after, 40, 147; unhabituated reactions to, 39, 40

September 11th Fund, 49

sexual abuse, 56

sexual issues and sexuality, 114; fear brokers' use of, 179–81

Sharvit, Keren, 36

Shaw, Artie, 107

Shelley, Percy Bysshe, 169
Siberia, Soviet labor camps in, 103
Silicio, Tami, 119
Simpson, John, 35
Small Kindness, 49
social cognition, 73
Sociopath Next Door, The (Stout), 75, 173
sociopaths, 15
sociopathy, 173
Soviet Union, 103–104, 110
spousal abuse, 120–33; case study, 122–33
Stalin, Joseph, 103
State Department, McCarthyism and, 105
Stevens, Cat (Yusuf Islam), 47–50, 61
Stevens, Robert, 108
Stone, Geoffrey R., 161–62
Strasser, Steven, 196
Struggle Till Dawn, 200
Supreme Court, U.S., 101–102

Tel Aviv University, 36
tellable stories, 52
temperament, inborn versus learned, 152–53
terrorism, 62, 120; courage as weapon against, 132, 143, 189, 201; definition of, 27; fear as weapon of, see fear, as weapon of terrorism; fear brokers, susceptibility to, see fear brokers; habituation to, 37–39; historical record of, 42; individual risk, 32, 190–92; motivations of terrorists, 21–23; national security, see national security; oversimplifying, 21–23; paranoia switch triggered by, see paranoia switch; as permanent phenomenon, 44, 141–42, 190, 191; personal worst-case scenarios, 192–93; safety signals and, 43–44; secrecy and, 117; successful, effects of, 24–34; unsuccessful acts of, 21, 22, 24, 34–37; see also specific types of and instances of terrorism
Terrorism and U.S. Foreign Policy (Pillar), 28
"Terrorism and You—The Real Odds," 191
Terrorism Information and Prevention System ("Operation TIPS"), 161
thalamus, 51
Thoreau, Henry David, 107, 165
torture, 195–99
trauma: causes of, see specific causes; definition of a traumatic event, 57; neurological record

trauma (*cont.*)
  of, *see* paranoia switch; neurological response to, 5–6, 8,
  86–87; process of recovery, 8;
  transgenerational effects of, *see*
  limbic resonance; traumatic
  memory, 52–57, 60; *see also*
  fear

University of Edinburgh, 10
University of North Carolina,
  166
University of Washington, Office
  of Financial Management,
  182
USA PATRIOT Act, 160–61
U.S. Department of Education,
  166
U.S. Information Service, 107,
  165

Vietnam War, 161
visualization, 87, 91

Walking-Around Anxiety Test,
  The, 16–19
Wallis, Jim, 164

war on terrorism, 110; civil
  liberties and, 160–61, 199;
  national security, *see* national
  security; *see also* September 11,
  2001
Washington Post, The, 32, 161,
  191
Wayne University, Brain Imaging Research Division of,
  76
Welles, Orson, 107
Wilson-Patterson Attitude Inventory
  (W-P), 153–54
worker's block, 31, 183
World War I, civil liberties during, 162
World War II, 102–103; internment of Japanese-Americans,
  see Japanese-Americans, internment of; Red Scare and
  McCarthyism, 103–109, 110,
  112, 114, 115, 118, 165, 170–
  72, 180–81, 186, 190
WTC Uncut, 59

Yehuda, Rachel, 27

Zakay, Dan, 36